God's Needle

Also by John Butterworth:

God's Secret Listener
Four Centuries at the Lion Hotel

God's Needle

How Lily Gaynor brought hope and healing
to the land of the witchdoctors

Lily Gaynor and

John Butterworth

MONARCH
BOOKS

Oxford, UK & Grand Rapids, Michigan, USA

Published by Monarch Books
an imprint of
Lion Hudson plc
Wilkinson House, Jordan Hill Road,
Oxford OX2 8DR, England
Email: monarch@lionhudson.com
www.lionhudson.com/monarch

ISBN 978 0 85721 456 0
e-ISBN 978 0 85721 457 7

First edition 2013

Acknowledgments
Scripture quotations taken from the *Holy Bible, New International Version*,
copyright © 1973, 1978, 1984 International Bible Society. Used by
permission of Hodder & Stoughton, a member of the Hodder Headline
Group. All rights reserved. "NIV" is a trademark of International Bible
Society. UK trademark number 1448790.
Extracts marked "KJV" are from The Authorized (King James) Version.
Rights in the Authorized Version are vested in the Crown. Reproduced by
permission of the Crown's patentee, Cambridge University Press.
Scripture marked "NKJV" taken from the New King James Version.
Copyright © 1982 by Thomas Nelson, Inc. Used by permission. All rights
reserved.
Scripture marked "NLT" taken from the Holy Bible, New Living
Translation, copyright © 1996, 2004, 2007 by Tyndale House Foundation.
Used by permission of Tyndale House Publishers, Inc., Carol Stream, Illinois
60188. All rights reserved.

Co-published with WEC.

A catalogue record for this book is available from the British Library

Printed and bound in the UK, June 2013, LH26

Dedicated to the enduring memory of Brenda Couche, Betty Dutch, and Pastor Domingos Gomes, who have supported, encouraged, and richly blessed me all through the years. They now have their reward!

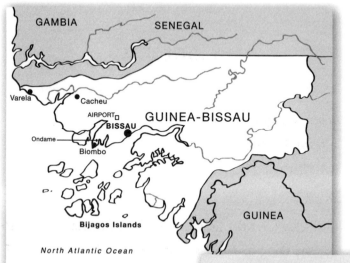

Contents

Acknowledgments

I would like to thank John Butterworth, for spending many hours researching and editing the manuscript; Stephen Power, for sorting out my computer problems again and again; and Marjorie Broughton and Thelma Mills, for helping my failing memory. Thanks are also due to my fellow members of Spellow Lane Church, Liverpool, for all their support, prayer, and encouragement. Finally, a special thank you goes to the WEC Fellowship here and in Africa, to whom I owe so much.

Foreword

When I was sent the manuscript, and asked if I would write a paragraph of recommendation, I hesitated – could I really take on another task? But then I glanced at the first chapter – and I was hooked! I simply couldn't put it down. It was exactly like reading my own story all over again. Lily went to West Africa just four years after I sailed for Congo... but what she met was so utterly similar to what I met, I was fascinated.

"Can I have God's needle?" – yes! There was the same utter confidence in the "needle" that they believed could and would heal any and every disease... it didn't really matter what you put in the syringe.

Then there was the overwhelming sense of personal incompetence – inadequacy – inability to cope. Everyone looked to you as though you were God, and thought you had the answer to every problem; added to that, there's the weariness – the need for a co-worker to share the burdens with, to discuss cases with. With the weariness often came the sense of inadequacy. All these things brought back such immediate memories of my own early days in Africa.

But at the same time I was reminded of the sheer joy of being there – the realization of the people's needs and

God's gracious love in sending you to meet those needs – especially the privilege of sharing the gospel with these dear people. What a privilege sharing the wonderful story of Jesus – of His birth, life, death, and resurrection, all for us – with a people who had never heard before!

As Lily's story unfolds, may the Lord speak into every heart. Here is a picture, in vivid colour, of what God has been graciously doing through the past hundred years of reaching out to tribal peoples all over the world with the gospel – using ordinary people, like you and me. Throughout this story, we see the Holy Spirit at work, changing Lily into the person God wanted her to be – conforming her to the image of His Son, Jesus. It calls to mind the verse from Philippians: "Not that I have already obtained all this, or have already arrived at my goal, but I press on…" (3:12).

This picture is not an accurate one, perhaps, of today's missionary efforts – often in countries now liberated from different forms of colonialism, and with leadership able to cope with the basic needs of their peoples. But it is a wonderful record of what was achieved to give a solid foundation for today's efforts. Lily's outpoured love and energy for the Papel people has left them with a church of believers, the basis of a medical service, and the written Word of God. To God be all the glory!

Helen Roseveare
September 2012

Introduction

Even seasoned travellers would probably be hard pressed to place Guinea-Bissau on a map of Africa. One of the most westerly countries on the continent, it is bordered by Senegal in the north and, to add to the confusion, another country called Guinea in the south. It is slightly larger in area than Belgium, but its population of 1.6 million is only a sixth of that of the European country.

This former colony of Portuguese Guinea, now called Guinea-Bissau, had one of the largest slave markets in the region based at Cacheu, which was known as the "Slave Coast", in the north-west of the country. Now it has swapped Cacheu for cashew nuts as its main source of revenue, as well as exporting fish and tropical hardwoods.

But it is still one of the poorest countries in the world, where even today in rural areas more than half the people do not have clean drinking water, and two-thirds do not have adequate sanitation. The country was not helped by an eleven-year war for independence from 1963 to 1974 and political instability since then, including a damaging civil war in the late 1990s. In 2008 it was ranked 175 out of 177 countries for poverty and had an 80 per cent infant mortality rate. Education is still a big problem, with only 13 per cent of secondary-age girls enrolled in school.

But there is cautious optimism about the future. Despite the lack of infrastructure some intrepid tourists are beginning to visit, no doubt encouraged by the *Lonely Planet* series, which recommends visiting the country in its *West Africa* travel guide. Two of the "must visits", it says, include the capital, Bissau, and the "remarkable" Arquipélago dos Bijagos islands. Of the capital it says: "Despite ruined monuments, cavernous potholes and regular blackouts, Bissau has its charms. The sleepy, crumbling colonial heart boasts wide, mango-shaded streets, some attractive, pastel-coloured buildings, and lively cafés where the country's elite gather day after day." It says the delta islands are "lined with powdery, white-sand beaches, washed by azure waters, and populated by a people whose matriarchal culture, long protected by hidden sandbanks and treacherous tides, is unlike any found in West Africa." By contrast, the mainland "provides a fine recapitulation of West Africa's attractions, including mangrove-lined rivers, a gorgeous beach at Varela and rainforests in the south – home to elephants and chimpanzees."

But many, many years before twenty-first-century adventurers flew in to the country, a young, thirty-year-old Liverpool lady, Lily Gaynor, arrived in the then Portuguese Guinea on Wednesday, 20 November 1957, after a ten-day boat journey from Portugal.

She had spent the previous twelve months learning Portuguese to prepare her to work among the Papel tribe in the remote west of the country.

Lily went with WEC International, a missionary organization that aimed to reach the least evangelized people in the world and whose motto is "If Jesus Christ be God and died for me, then no sacrifice can be too great for me to make for him."

WEC was founded in 1913 by the England cricketer Charles Thomas Studd, who had played in the 1882 match, which Australia won, and was the start of The Ashes series.

After serving Christ in China and India, 53-year-old C. T. Studd felt God calling him to pioneer a new worldwide mission and, despite suspect health, set sail for Africa. Before he died in the Belgian Congo in 1931, teams of missionaries had joined WEC to work in Central and West Africa, Amazonia, the Middle East, and the Himalayan region. Today there are 1,800 workers from more than fifty nationalities serving in multi-cultural teams among ninety of the least evangelized people groups.

Among those who followed in C. T. Studd's footsteps was Lily, who spent thirty-five years working among the Papel tribe, one of twenty-seven ethnic groups in the country, and whose language had never even been written down. Despite failing her 11 plus Lily became a highly qualified nurse and midwife and an accomplished linguist. She turned her back on a promising career in England to live in an African hut in the village of Ondame in the remote area of Biombo.

In the mornings she took a chair and table out under the mango trees where she held medical clinics six days a week that proved a huge success thanks to the penicillin injection or, as villagers preferred to call it, "God's needle". In the afternoons she visited the villages to learn Papel, where she came into contact with the greatly feared witchdoctors. In the evenings she invented a written alphabet so she could translate the New Testament into their language.

Today the country, renamed Guinea-Bissau after independence, has one of the biggest national churches in West Africa. This is Lily's story, or as she prefers to say, this is His story.

Chapter 1

Please Give the Dead Mum God's Needle

"Senhora! Senhora! SENHORA!" Each time it got louder as it penetrated my sleep.

"What is it?" I shouted.

"It's bad, very bad – she's had the baby but it is bad. Come quickly."

I fished under the pillow for my torch, crawled from under the mosquito net, pulled on my plastic sandals and a dress over my nightdress, and lit the small paraffin lantern. I collected my midwifery bag, left my mud hut, and went out into the moonless, hot African night. It was well after midnight in the little-known republic, now called Guinea-Bissau, on the west coast of this great continent.

Outside two anxious men were eager to move off. Each was barefoot, wearing only the usual loin cloth and carrying a vicious-looking machete. As I walked between them along the narrow bush path, my lantern was giving out a feeble circle of light, enough to see the rough stony path, but still I worried about the snakes and the hyenas. On the other hand, such night trips always gave me a thrill – the stillness, the continual chorus of crickets and frogs, the beat, beat of drums in the distance telling of another funeral, and the occasional mating laugh of a hyena. This fleeting pleasure was sobered by the fear of what awaited me and the abysmal inadequacy I always felt in these emergencies.

After a half-hour's walk we entered the small, round mud hut in a remote village near the coastal area of Biombo. The only light was from a flickering wood fire in the middle of the room. My eyes were smarting from the smoke, but I was able to make out several women seated on the floor, leaning against the bare mud wall. There was complete silence except for a grunt from a pig in a corner, and a flutter from the hens perched overhead. Then I saw a girl, presumably the mother, sitting on the dirt floor in a pool of mud and blood. She was leaning back, held in the lap of another woman. A baby lay face down in the quagmire between her knees. I picked the baby up, realizing that he was alive, though very cold. The cord was still intact, so I separated it quickly, wrapped him in a towel and pressed him against the bosom of one of the ladies. She tried to refuse, but I had no time, nor patience, to argue!

I turned to the mother; she looked young, probably about fourteen. Her face was grey, and as I laid my hand on her arm I felt, with horror, the cold stiffening flesh of someone who had been dead for a while. I looked up at the two men who had brought me, and round at the other women. No word was spoken, just complete silence. I could hardly speak. "She has been dead for some time," I ventured. "Did you not know?"

"Yes, Senhora," one of the men replied, "but we wanted you to come."

"What can I do now? You should have called me earlier. I might have been able to save her then," I said, though I knew this reasoning was hopeless.

"Oh no, Senhora," he said emphatically, "please give her *guja Kristu* [God's needle and penicillin] and bring her back to life."

What could I say? Desperation overwhelmed me. "Only God can do that, only Jesus can give life," I stammered, fighting back the tears, but words were not enough.

I did what I could and left the villagers to look after the baby and to bury his mother.

As the men kindly accompanied me home, walking in the darkness now seemed so oppressive and overpowering. I argued with the Lord: "Why am I here? It's all so hopeless. I am totally inadequate."

"What about the baby?" I continued. I knew that no woman would take him as they think the dead mother will need the baby to suck on her swollen breasts and so will curse anybody who keeps her baby from her. "Has he to die, as so many babies and other mothers die so needlessly?" I cried out in the darkness.

"God, where is the fulfilment of your promises to me? All these people ever want is Christ's needle. Why is there so little response to the gospel?"

I had no idea at that time that Alexander Fleming, the inventor of penicillin, and the *guja*, or "needle", was a vital part of God's plan for one tiny tribe in this almost totally unheard-of country.

It was 4.30 in the morning when I eventually returned to my bed. I was utterly exhausted. A mosquito had managed to get under the mosquito net with me. But I was too tired to find and swat it as I stumbled back to sleep wondering why I had swapped a comfortable Merseyside home for a mud hut in Africa.

Chapter 2

The Long-haired Lass from Liverpool

"Mummy," I cried, "how do you make soap?"

"I don't make it; I buy it," she replied.

"A missionary taught the African chief how to make soap and they all became Christians," I explained. "So I want to know how to make soap, because I'm going to be a missionary when I grow up."

It was 1935 and I was eight when I came home excitedly one day from the little church, Orrell Park Presbyterian, opposite my home in Bailey Drive, Bootle. Today that church is St Stephen's United Reformed Church. It had been a special meeting, where a missionary had shown magic-lantern pictures of Africa. It was so exciting! I had been at the church since being on the "Cradle Roll" when I was three years old. Though my parents, John and Edith, never went to church themselves, they insisted that I did. So I was sent to the 11 a.m. service, which included a children's talk; Sunday school at 2 p.m. and a 6.30 p.m. gospel service, which I really liked. The singing was led by Miss Mayman who played the piano. I was fascinated watching her play the choruses from different music books, thinking, "However can she do it?" The words didn't mean a thing at the time, but it was there that my journey to faith began.

Times were hard in the 1930s. Dad, in the building trade, was often out of work. In order to get some money he would push his handcart with his ladders up to 10 miles to the other side of Liverpool to paper and paint a room for a pittance. I had two early lessons in how precious money was then. First, as a youngster I was always saying, "I want... Buy me..." when out shopping with my mum. Eventually, she said angrily, "We haven't enough money for food. If you say 'I want' one more time I'll smack your bottom." I did and she did. She pulled my knickers down and slapped me there in the street. I've never been so humiliated!

My second lesson in money came from our neighbours. The man next door always seemed so posh wearing a trilby hat and a suit and carrying a mackintosh and an umbrella. One day my mum discovered the respectable man's wife next door lying on her bed, dying of starvation. She was shocked to find that there was nothing to eat in her house. Mum made her have some porridge, and then persuaded her to take the 9 shillings (45p) a week dole money, which she had been too proud to apply for previously. Life then improved considerably for the neighbours.

* * *

On the whole my childhood was a happy one. I was possibly spoilt because I was an only child and because I had suffered ill health. When I was seven years old I spent three months in hospital where I had scarlet fever, diphtheria, measles, and then appendicitis. It didn't help that visitors were allowed only on Sundays. Throughout my long stay in hospital I admired the nurses for the help and care they gave to me and the other patients. It was then that I realized I wanted to be a nurse one day.

When I went back home I used to enjoy going to the store at the back of the nearby market where I could gaze at the lovely puppies for sale. One Christmas morning, as the gifts were spread on my bed, Mum said, "Go and see what Father Christmas has brought you downstairs." In the kitchen I found – joy of joys – a puppy, which I called Timmy. In the afternoon, when we trudged through the snow to Nana and Granddad's house round the corner, Timmy had to go too. He added to the chaos of cousins, aunts, and uncles in their small semi-detached home. From that day on I have never been without a dog in my life.

On my eighth birthday on 12 July 1935, when Dad was out of work again, my parents gave me a new Brownie uniform. Of course, I didn't realize at the time just how much it cost them and all the love that was wrapped up in that brown paper parcel. It was the beginning of years of excitement through Brownies, Guides, and Sea Rangers. We enjoyed summer and weekend camping trips, and rowing a six-oared boat on the dirty Leeds and Liverpool Canal, accompanied by naughty boys running on the footpath shouting and throwing stones in the water.

Despite the economic hardship we still had a family holiday every year when we went camping at nearby Formby for five weeks in the summer. It meant a train journey and a $1^1/_2$-mile walk at the other end, carrying all our equipment and food. Timmy came with us, but my dad visited us only at weekends as he had to work in the week.

In 1938 I took the 11-plus scholarship. On the day of the exam I came home at lunchtime and told my mum I didn't feel very well. She insisted I went back, but when I returned home that evening I was covered in spots and discovered I had chickenpox. Not surprisingly I failed the exam and so couldn't go to the local grammar school. Mum was sad because her hopes of her only child rising above the poverty of the working class were dashed, and I was upset because I was going to be separated from my best friend, Joyce Nelson, who had passed the 11 plus. Sadly, Joyce and I fell out. I started it by calling her "stuck-up", to which she would reply, "You're only jealous!" Doubtless she was right.

At the same time I was feeling unhappy. I couldn't sleep at night because I was ridden with guilt and shame. My school work suffered, my health deteriorated, and when I went into the senior elementary of Roberts Council School I came thirty-fifth in a class of forty girls. My grandmother said it was because my strength was going into my long hair and I should have it cut. I knew it wasn't because of my long hair; it was because of my guilt and shame after a seventeen-year-old youth had sexually assaulted me a year earlier.

But then, a few months later, on 12 April 1939, my life changed for ever! I was in bed trying to get to sleep. I recited poetry to myself; I sang songs we learned at school and choruses from Sunday school, but sleep didn't come. Then, unexpectedly, something far more wonderful did! I sang the chorus:

> Rolled away, rolled away, and the burden of my heart rolled away.
> Every sin had to go beneath the cleansing flow.
> Hallelujah…

Like a brilliant light suddenly being turned on, I realized what those words meant. It was as if, in an instant, all the teaching of years in Sunday school unravelled in my brain. Jesus became real. I just knew what the cross meant: Jesus died – and it was for me. Forgiveness! To be made clean! In floods of tears I leapt out of bed, knelt down, and cried, "Take it away, God; please take it away." He did – and I knew it. The guilt and fear had gone. I felt washed clean. I went to my window and there saw the night sky as I'd never seen it before. It was glorious, rapturous. Everything was new and wonderful.

I needed no counsellor after the assault, though in those days that sort of help wasn't available anyway. Jesus was my Counsellor. I had fallen in love with Him. No more insomnia. In fact, my mum couldn't make out why I was now in a hurry to go to bed: it was because that was when I talked to Jesus. I didn't know that prayer could be at any time of the day or night.

At the end of the summer term at school I was top of the class, and stayed in the top four for the rest of my schooling. This was despite being evacuated to Southport, well away from the Liverpool Docks, which were a target for the German bombers now war had broken out. But my mum missed me so much she brought me home early, interrupting my schooling even more. I was sad my education finished when I was fourteen. But I was glad I never had to have my long hair cut because my mum later let me have it in a grown-up style!

Chapter 3

From Delivering Milk to Delivering Babies

It was 1941 and wartime when I left school and started work. At great sacrifice my parents insisted I take an expensive secretarial course, which at the time I didn't appreciate at all, though learning to touch-type and some elementary book-keeping proved to be useful later. I got a junior clerk's job in the Co-op Insurance at the age of fourteen, but I hated my three years there. I only wanted to be a nurse, but my parents wouldn't listen to me.

To help the war effort Mum pushed a large milk cart around the district, starting at 5 a.m. every day. Each Saturday and Sunday I helped her with the deliveries, and in the afternoons I collected the money. I did that willingly, as sometimes the women gave me an extra penny. But with working all day on Sundays I forgot about the little Presbyterian church I had attended as a child. I lost contact with Christians, rarely prayed, and as my initial zeal wore off, any thoughts of being a missionary faded.

Every night we had to put our wellington boots on and go down to the Anderson shelter at the bottom of our garden where there were two bunks and up to 12 inches of water.

Although we were a few miles away from the centre of Liverpool, we could hear the bombs landing all along the docklands area.

During the war my dad, who later spent two years with the RAF in India, joined the Rescue Squad to help people trapped in bombed houses and buildings in Bootle. I put on my Guide uniform and offered to help him, but Mum wouldn't let me go with him!

Dad was nearly called up for action in our own house when a stray incendiary bomb came through our roof and lodged in my bedroom wardrobe without exploding. Fortunately, Mum and I were in the garden shelter at the time.

However, I still longed to be a nurse. So with female guile I played on Mum's patriotism and she allowed me to help the "War Effort" by being an assistant nurse at Belmont Road Hospital in Anfield, Liverpool. I was able to live at home, while the nurses in training had to stay at the hospital. I was assigned to the third floor of the women's ward – there was no lift in those days. We had thirty severe stroke patients, who were all incontinent and paralysed; some were unconscious and tube-fed. My long days were spent changing beds, cleaning bottoms, and running up and down the three flights to get the sheets and to collect the food that had to be forced down these pitiful patients. The job was heart-wrenching, but I loved it.

A few weeks later I passed the acceptance exam and proudly became an assistant nurse. How I loved to show off my uniform as I travelled on the bus. I was thrilled when I was transferred to Walton General Hospital in Liverpool, which was nearer to home and gave me a much wider experience of nursing. Sadly, after about a year my mum became very ill and I had to give up the job. I was needed to care for her and to help Dad in the shop he had bought with his demob money from the Air Force. Selling wallpaper and paint was certainly not my line. Mum recovered and I longed to be able to return to nursing, but how could I leave them in the lurch?

In 1947 Dad said to me out of the blue one day as we sat at the tea table, "If you want to go and train to be a qualified nurse, then go. But I guarantee you'll be back home within three months."

Within a fortnight I was a student nurse at Walton Hospital, Liverpool, living in the nurses' home. I revelled in the 48-hour week; I put up with the big drop in my salary to £3 a month, and I coped with the inadequate food by going home on my day off each week. I enjoyed the community living, the studies, and the camaraderie. I was free – and I loved the job. But deep in my subconscious, hidden for many years, was the desire to be a missionary. Some student nurses befriended me. They talked about being "born again" and "converted", terms which were new to me, but I began to realize that was what had happened to me in 1939. I loved the Nurses' Christian Fellowship meetings and the friendships that grew from it, especially a very handsome and lovely boyfriend and sweet dreams of the future. Life was wonderful!

On 12 July 1948, my twenty-first birthday, I had a great party with relatives and friends and lots of presents. As I went to bed that night I prayed and thanked God. I thought, "Perhaps God will give me a birthday present too." He did. I opened my Bible at random and dropped my finger on a verse: "Ask of me and I shall give thee the heathen for thine inheritance..." (Psalm 2:8, KJV).

Of course, it is entirely out of context, but I didn't know that at the time. It was a word from God to me personally. All my childhood dreams came flooding back. "A missionary," I thought. "Yes me, yes me! God's twenty-first birthday gift to me. Wow!"

* * *

A year's midwifery training followed the general nursing training. I enjoyed it so much that I began to think I would rather be a midwifery tutor than go abroad. Training as a nurse had taught me what it meant to leave my family, friends, and home comforts – necessary sacrifices for any missionary. But missionary meetings made me uncomfortable, especially a very zealous couple, Ted and Ethel Bushell, who were the Liverpool representatives of what I thought at first was a strange, way-out society called the Worldwide Evangelisation Crusade, now known as WEC International. The Bushells had a burden for nurses – and I was irresistibly drawn to their prayer meetings. But the more I learnt about this faith mission that didn't appeal for money and that every WEC missionary trusted God for all their needs, the scarier it became – and the less confident I was that I could ever do that.

My next step in nursing was a six-month tropical medical diploma at the University College Hospital in London. It was exciting, especially when I found that the nurse in the next bedroom was a Christian, Eva Beresford. To my amazement she was on her way to the Belgian Congo as a missionary with that same weird mission, WEC. She scared me stiff with stories about Bible College and the training.

One day Eva challenged me: "The Lord is calling you to be a missionary. Why don't you send for the application forms for Bible School?"

"Oh no," I replied quickly, "I did think that once, but now I know I couldn't do it. I haven't that sort of faith, nor the education. It is not for me."

"Go and tell all those reasons to the Lord," she said, and walked away.

So I did. Alone in my room, on my knees, I poured out all my fears, doubts, and inadequacies to Jesus. It wasn't long before I gave in, weeping and still afraid. I cried out, "If this is really Your will, Lord, please show me Your glory now."

He did! The sudden, precious sense of the presence of Jesus was beyond words. His love poured over me in waves. Tears of doubt and fear turned to tears of joy and relief.

I wrote that night to the WEC Bible College in Glasgow and received the application forms within a few days.

My joy quickly evaporated as I answered some of the questions on the form:

Have your read the Bible through? **No**

Have you won anyone to Christ? **No**

Do your parents approve of you being a missionary? **No**

What educational qualifications do you have? **None**

Are you prepared to trust the Lord for all your needs? **Not yet**

I hoped that my lack of faith would change in two years' time when I would finish Bible School.

"Well, that's that," I thought as I posted it. "I'll be a midwifery tutor after all." A few days later a letter arrived telling me to report to the Glasgow college on 6 October 1953.

Chapter 4

First Stop Portugal, then Portuguese Guinea

I had six months to wait before Bible College, so I worked at St Paul's Eye Hospital to gain more nursing experience. There I met Sister Betty Dutch, who became a faithful friend, supporter, and my lifeline for fifty years, and also Brenda Couche, who later became my co-worker and precious friend. I was able to save enough money for my first term at college. I kept it in an Elastoplast tin, counting it frequently, until I reckoned that, together with the superannuation from nursing, it would cover my fees for the first year. Again the Lord thought differently.

I was at an August bank holiday Bible conference at Emmanuel Bible College, Birkenhead, where the congregation was told that we would present our offerings at the final meeting. I was no "cheerful giver", but I joined the queue going to the front where I deposited the red tin containing £62 in the basket. It looked so conspicuous among the money. That was an enormous amount to me, and the first time I had ever given money sacrificially. It hurt so much, but somehow the fear of all that lay ahead vanished. How I hung on to that promise of Luke 6:38 –

"Give, and it will be given to you" – as I set out for my first term at Bible College.

I was completely out of my depth in my exams, and spent much of the first week in tears.

There was an IQ test which I thought I had messed up. An English grammar assessment test followed. There were five questions; I could answer only one and I got that wrong.

My first assignment was "A chronological account of the life and work of Jesus, using only the Bible". I messed that up too. The principal, Stewart Dinnen, marked the assignment as C-, but with a red note at the end: "With your IQ you can do much better than this." I couldn't believe it. He actually thinks I can make it, I thought. It was such an encouragement.

***

Another first-year student, Isa Arthur, and I were out on compulsory visitation one afternoon in a deprived part of Glasgow. We were trying to sell books and talk to people about the gospel. As we knocked on each door I found myself praying that no one would be in. It was agony. "We haven't done very well, have we?" Isa said that evening. "Why don't we pray about it?"

As we discussed our fears and hopelessness we both felt that there must be something more. We needed the Holy Spirit in a new way, and we knew it. So that night, after "Lights Out", we crept up to the top floor, into a cubbyhole where the brushes and buckets were kept. There was just enough room for us to stand up. We had decided to pray until the Lord met with us, even if it took all night. I wasn't coping and felt that I needed to meet with Jesus in a new way.

"Perhaps it is this baptism of the Spirit that some people talk about," I suggested to Isa, but she didn't know either. After several hours of muddled, incoherent praying and waiting, Isa opened her Bible and read: "Let anyone who is thirsty come to me and drink. Whoever believes in me… rivers of living water will flow from within them" (John 7:37–38).

"That's us," Isa said. "We've just got to drink in faith. Yes?"

"How do we do that?" I asked.

After a pause she said, "I don't know but I'll try it." She took a deep breath and said, "Lord Jesus, I am drinking now and believe your promise." I took a step of faith and followed. I had to do something; Isa wasn't going to move until I did!

Nothing happened. I didn't know what I was expecting. Whatever it was it didn't happen. However, the rain that had been falling gently on the skylight above our heads suddenly became a deluge. To me it seemed so significant and, to quote my diary of that time, "I drank and drank of that life-giving stream."

"We can go to bed now," said Isa. So we did. It was half past one in the morning.

Next morning I woke with an overwhelming sense that something had happened after all.

Jesus was real in a way I had never experienced before. To say there was a change in me was an understatement.

The timidity and self-doubt had gone. The Bible opened up like a great treasure. Hymns became so meaningful they brought tears to my eyes. I wanted to tell everybody. I became aware of sins in me that I had never been aware of and they had to be confessed and put right immediately.

The two years in Bible College became a joy and all my fees were paid for somehow. On one occasion when I was returning to Glasgow after a holiday, I needed £1 for the coach journey. As I had only a few pence I decided to take a bus to Ormskirk and hitch-hike from there. My dad went to the bus stop with me, having no idea that I wasn't already booked on a coach from Ormskirk. As he said goodbye, he pressed a note into my hand, saying, with a big grin, "This is from me. It isn't from the Lord." I could have answered, "It's from both of you", but I wasn't quick enough. It was £5, more than enough for all my needs. Trusting the Lord for the finances, for my fees for the two years in Bible College and the fees for the Wycliffe language course, travel, and all the expenses involved proved not only to be a challenge, but also exciting, as time and time again there was a cliffhanger and a miracle.

I had other things I needed to learn that were painful. In my second year I wrote in my diary:

> He has brought me through the most precious
> experience of my life. All last week the
> conviction of sin has deepened. God laid bare
> all the deception and sin of my heart until each
> prayer time became agony. Each night I cried
> out for cleansing in the blood of Jesus, but I

got no peace and wept and wept. Each day it seemed my sin was mounting.

Last week I was challenged to confess my pride and sin openly to the whole fellowship, but I just couldn't bring myself to do it. In desperation, I just handed Jesus the key to open the sluice gates. Immediately my soul was flooded with relief and joy. I knew just what I had to do. I went into the fellowship meeting promising God that I would obey.

I wasn't really surprised when the visiting speaker preached about victory through brokenness and open confession. It was so obviously straight from God to me. There were several confessions by others that gave me the courage to speak out. I knew I had to say sorry for all that He had put His finger on: my pride at being made head student, how I thought that I was the best person for the position, my glorying in souls won, and making sure, in a subtle way, that people knew about it. The Holy Spirit prompted me through the tears – God knows what I really am, so everyone else might as well know.

At Bible College I was particularly challenged when a missionary came to visit us from the tiny West African country that was then called Portuguese Guinea. He spoke of whole tribes unaware of the gospel and who had no medical help at all. Only a small team of missionaries were working in three of the twenty-seven tribes. I felt as if I was already there and not just one of the forty students in the hall. I struggled with this for weeks. The slides he had shown kept appearing in my mind. Was God really speaking to me? I was a bit anxious in case I was being influenced because my friend Isa was heading for that country as well.

✳ ✳ ✳

After a further six months as a candidate in the WEC Headquarters, and a linguistic course at Wycliffe Bible Translators, I was finally accepted into the WEC mission with the idea of going to what is now Guinea-Bissau. First, however, I was given the go-ahead to go to Portugal to learn Portuguese to prepare for West Africa.

The only problem was that I had to have £100 before I could leave. They might as well have said £1,000. For six months I began to wonder whether I had made a mistake, so I asked the Lord to send me something in the post that day. He sent £10. That was enough to quench my doubts. There was a sailing in five weeks' time, so I went to Fred, our business secretary, and asked him to book the passage for me. "How much money do you have?" he asked. "Ten pounds," I answered. Without a flicker of a smile he said, "You'll need only another £90 before I can book it."

For the formidable equipment I needed I was advised to go to Dakins, a big wholesale firm that supplied medicines and medical equipment to missions and overseas charities at lower prices. Go to the top, I was told. So, with fear and reluctance I went into the awesome offices in London and asked for the tropical department manager. I showed him my list and asked him to price it. He smiled at me, saying, "Do you mind if I ask how much money you can spend?"

"About £5," I answered. His eyebrows shot up. So I decided my faith had better shoot up too. "Well, £10," I said, taking a leap of faith.

His eyebrows stayed up, but he went through my list, including medicines, injections, and some expensive instruments. He suggested cheaper alternatives and made many practical suggestions. In later years our Dakins' bills were in the hundreds of pounds.

Tackling the other items on the equipment list needed more miracles. It included mosquito boots that went up to the knees, an Aladdin lamp, a saw for ladies, an appropriate swimming costume, and tin trunks – because of crocodiles, I thought! Wherever would I get a canvas bath and wash basin and a pith helmet? But they were all provided for, including the abominable pith helmet, which was an ugly-looking cork headgear that I was supposed to wear all the time.

Then, out of the blue, to help me on my way a £50 cheque came in the post from a WEC missionary in Thailand, to whom I had never written, and I don't think she knew of my need. My dad sent £50, again telling me that it was from Mum and him and not from the Lord, and the rest of the money arrived. So, on 16 November 1956 I set sail from Liverpool with a big send-off from my parents, other family members, and friends. I was off. Goodbye, England! Next stop Portugal, for a year, and then Portuguese Guinea.

Chapter 5

What the Duke of Edinburgh Said to Me

I had three days in luxury as I travelled to Lisbon with the idle rich on a cruise ship. I must have looked like the poor relation in comparison.

I lived in Almada, on the other side of the River Tagus to Lisbon, with an English Brethren family who were very good to me, treating me as one of them and even occasionally taking me on outings. My time was spent in language study, with three hours a week private tuition, and I also enrolled for a three-month nursing course at the local university.

I was advised to put enough money in the bank for my onward journey to West Africa. So I banked £50 and lived on the remainder, which just paid for my digs and lessons for three months with not much left over. There were other would-be missionaries like me having language lessons too. But they were mostly Americans, and money for them seemed to be plentiful. I felt the poor relation again, just as I had on the cruise ship. Time and again I was invited to go sightseeing with them on Saturdays, but on each occasion I said that I needed to study. I just didn't have the money, but I couldn't say so. I became a real "Holier than thou" in their eyes and stuck out like a sore thumb. It wasn't nice. I had, and still have, an inordinate desire to be liked.

One day they went to a beach near my digs for a picnic lunch so I could accept their invitation, as my kindly landlady supplied the food. Then, to my horror, at lunchtime they all decided to go to a hotel for a proper lunch – and fed their picnics to the seagulls. If I had said that I had no money I am sure they would have treated me. But I couldn't do that, so I lied and told them I had to go back home. I had a miserable, lonely picnic hiding in the sand dunes, imagining the slap-up lunch, the jolly fellowship, and, sadly, also imagining some uncomplimentary comments about me.

The money became so tight that I had to withdraw the £50 I had banked for the voyage to Portuguese Guinea. It lasted only about three more months, and then there was a nervous moment every time when I paid for my digs in advance. Each month my anxious prayers were answered miraculously, with exactly what I needed. Then I was delighted to hear that my visa to go to Portuguese Guinea had been granted, but at the same time my visa to stay in Portugal expired, so I had to get out of the country as quickly as possible.

The following Monday I went to book my passage for the ten-day trip on the ship leaving on the following Sunday, 10 November 1957. I was told the ticket had to be paid for by Saturday noon the day before the ship sailed. But there was a big problem: no money. I remembered a plaque in the principal's office at Bible College that said, "The turtle gets nowhere until it sticks its neck out." I had indeed stuck my neck out and it was about to get the chop. I learnt a great deal about prayer in those six days. When it came to Friday I was thinking, "Should I cable my Dad?" He would have sent me money, not to go to Africa, but to go home.

Saturday morning dawned after a sleepless night. I could hardly believe my eyes when a letter arrived that morning from the Banco do Espirito Santo bank, which I had never heard of before, saying, "A remittance has been received for you. Please come and collect it." I had just enough money to get the ferry to cross the river to Lisbon, where I ran to the bank and signed for £64.

I then dashed to the shipping office, getting there at 11.40 a.m., only twenty minutes before my deadline. I paid £62 for my ticket and still had enough change to retrieve my watch from the repair shop, which I had been resigned to leaving in Portugal.

It was many years later before I found out that the money had come from England and was made up of smaller gifts from different people.

***

As I boarded the ship I looked back on my enjoyable year in Portugal and, in particular, two highlights. First, my mum and dad surprised me by coming out to see me over Christmas and New Year and took me to Portuguese places that I could never have afforded to go to on my own. At the end of the fortnight Dad gave me £20. Although I was touched by my parents' gift, I was even more pleased that their disapproval of me going to Portuguese Guinea as a missionary had gone completely.

The second highlight was Queen Elizabeth II's first visit to Portugal, 18–20 February 1957. The Queen had disembarked from the Royal Yacht moored in the Tagus and was reunited with Prince Philip after a four-month separation because of official duties. Apparently, the Duke of Edinburgh wore a tie with hearts on to celebrate the reunion.

The Portuguese state spared no expense, buying a carriage and Rolls-Royce to transport the Queen and the Duke to the Queluz National Palace, where they were staying. A banquet was held in their honour, and I and all the expatriate English in Lisbon received a large elaborate invitation to a reception at the palace.

It was formal dress, so I had to have either long sleeves or gloves with sleeves, plus stockings and a hat. We were told how to curtsy and to address Her Majesty as Ma'am, but only if she spoke to us. Many bought new dresses and hats for the occasion, but I managed to avoid joining in the talk and the shopping sprees. I had only one long-sleeved dress, which was a rather ancient navy blue one. I had also brought a pink hat out with me to Portugal to wear if I attended a Brethren church. My landlady didn't think too much of the old hat, but she produced some pretty pink net and made the hat look brand new. I bought a pair of pink silk gloves and a pink rose for the dress, and with my blonde hair and the hairdressing skills of a Portuguese friend I felt I looked good.

All the guests were lined up in two rows, one on each side of the long hall. We had a rehearsal on curtsying and further protocol instructions. When the Queen arrived she was followed by Prince Philip and the retinue. When she came to me she graciously shook my gloved hand and smiled and was about to move on. However, Prince Philip stopped and asked what I was doing in Lisbon.

"I'm here to learn Portuguese and go to Portuguese Guinea as a missionary," I replied, adding a "Sir". I hoped that was right as they had taught us how to address the Queen but not the Prince.

"Why aren't you going to an English colony?" he asked. I doubt he understood my unprepared answer about the Lord's leading.

As he went further along the line he met a Catholic priest who was also going to Portuguese Guinea as a missionary. The Duke of Edinburgh stopped the royal party, came back to me, and, pointing out the Catholic priest to me, said, "You two should get together now."

Chapter 6

Welcome to West Africa, Witchcraft, and Voodoo

The little Portuguese boat from Lisbon to Portuguese Guinea could not have been more different to the cruise ship that brought me from England to Portugal. This tub was not really geared up to take passengers and I had the doubtful privilege of being the only one.

I sat at the cramped captain's table with burly officers on either side of me, and breakfast was the same every morning for all ten days of the trip – kidneys floating in olive oil. If nothing else, it was good missionary training.

The ship put in at Praia in the Cape Verde Islands, so I eagerly opted to go ashore. I lived to regret it! It was relatively easy going down the ladder into a rowing boat, as I was helped by a kindly sailor. But I hadn't bargained for catching a rope ladder to get up on to the wharf. The sea was choppy, the little boat bounced up and down, and the ladder was always in the wrong place when it bounced up. When I finally scaled it, poking my head over the parapet, I found there was nothing to get hold of. I couldn't go down again as the rowing boat had gone. Heaving myself up also proved impossible. Thankfully, a big local man heard my anguished cries, knelt down and wrapped his strong arms around me, and hauled me up. I could have kissed him, but I thought I had better not.

I heard that there were English missionaries on that island, so I went to visit them expecting to get a decent meal. However, kind as they were, I was somewhat disappointed to find that it was their fast day, but they did give me a cup of lovely English tea and home-baked bread and butter. Then it was back to the ship for the kidneys!

***

It wasn't long before I arrived in Bissau, the lovely capital. It was very Portuguese with its white and colour-washed buildings, all bathed in brilliant sunshine. Palm trees and flowers abounded, and the market and shops were full of all kinds of African and Portuguese food. I was very impressed, but was soon to learn that life wasn't like this outside the city.

I was met by Leslie and Bessie Brierley, who were the first permanent Protestant missionaries in the country. The incredible story of Bessie, a waitress from the slums of London's East End, is told in the book *Going for God* (Hodder and Stoughton, 1972). Bessie arrived on her own in Portuguese Guinea on 20 May 1940, and stayed over a year until illness forced her to move to Freetown, Sierra Leone, where she met up again with Leslie Brierley. They married and were eventually allowed to return to Portuguese Guinea in 1945, where they stayed until 1959. They came back to work at WEC HQ in Bulstrode, England, for ten years before Bessie was killed and Leslie was badly injured in a car crash. Leslie, who became WEC's Research Secretary for many years, married again. He died on 18 July 2008.

Leslie had arranged that I should go to the Biombo area, the centre of the Papel tribe. "You are to learn the Papel language," he said. "Turn it into a written language and then translate the New Testament into Papel."

If he thought he was encouraging me he was mistaken. I quickly found that my limited knowledge of Portuguese was of little use, and I needed first to learn Creole before I could attempt Papel.

***

Two months later, in January 1958, I took my first trip on a decrepit African bus for the 40-mile journey to the Biombo region on a peninsula of mangrove swamps, 15 miles long and 2 miles wide with a population then of 16,000. I joined Val Esping, an American, who was the first Protestant missionary to go to the Papel people and had been there a few months. However, as she spoke only Portuguese she was more needed in Bissau and was soon moved back there. Nonetheless, the older missionary was an essential mentor for the short time we overlapped.

We lived in a tiny compound in the remote village of Ondame, with two straw-roofed mud houses. Surrounded by brilliant skies, warm sunshine, tall palm trees, and squat banana trees, there was no doubt I was in real Africa. If I needed reminding of that there was always the continual beat of the African drum in the background. Living there was like being in an open-air zoo as I could listen from the verandah to the constant chatter of tropical birds, many large and resplendent in brilliant red, blue, and green plumage. I could also watch the colourful butterflies flitting among the maize and peanut plants and the lush vegetation of the trees laden with palm nuts, mangoes, and papayas. I could have sat there for hours, if it wasn't for the mosquitoes that quickly drove me indoors.

Val had already done a good job in arranging everything we needed – a well with buckets and a rope, a barrel for the water, two small paraffin lanterns, a little charcoal stove to cook on, and a table with washing-up bowls and pots and pans. I had a single room where I put my camp bed and a tea chest that held all my possessions.

I was also shown the long-drop outside toilet. What more could I want? A toilet roll? Easy! Half-pages of a *Reader's Digest* with string threaded through them were ideal, except that I found it frustrating each time I tried to read an article and couldn't locate the other half-page. An extra problem was the large family of cockroaches that inhabited the hole and came up the toilet at night.

On one of my monthly trips to Bissau on the bus to do my shopping, collect the mail, and see other members of the mission, I decided to get one over the beasts in the toilet, and buy a potty. But when I was in the shop I didn't know what to call it in Portuguese. "Basin" was the nearest word I could come up with. So the shop assistant tried various types of basins and bowls. Eventually, with some gesticulations by me, which are better left unmentioned, he cried: "Ah! A basin for the bed." That wasn't the real name, but it served its purpose. I went back to the village triumphant with my precious treasure.

***

There was no time to acclimatize as I was thrown into African tribal life the first afternoon I arrived. An elderly man, a close neighbour, had died and the funeral was in full swing. "We've got to go to show our respects," Val explained. "It goes on for seven days or more and we have to go every day." It was horrendous!

On the way one of the local evangelists, José, took me inside the hut, which was both a centre for witchcraft and voodoo ceremonies – and the local hospital. It consisted of a grass roof set on poles. Inside, there was a bed for the patient, a hewn stone-slab bed for the priestess, a place for sacrifice, and a trough for the sacred water. Walking across the dirt road I passed a rusty half-petrol drum containing spirit pots with the offerings of rice and fire-water, a very potent alcoholic drink made from sugarcane, to appease the departed relatives. Nearby a broken gourd was tied up with some blood-stained red cloth, apparently to persuade the Iran, the chief ruling spirit, to cure a sick child.

At the funeral the beating of the drums, the noise, and the screaming were frightening. Women, dressed in just their loin cloths, danced wailing around the corpse lying on the ground wrapped in layers of cloths. A man arrayed in coils of rope and a scanty, far from adequate, goat skin, danced up to me. His black skin was plastered with white mud, and he held a vicious-looking machete over his shoulder. He put his face right up to mine; his eyes were bright red due to drinking all day and his breath stunk of the fire-water which he had in a bottle in his hand. He chanted something that was quite unintelligible to me. I was scared and backed off, but he moved closer still, until I was pinned trembling against the fence. I wondered whether he was just welcoming me. Or was he putting a curse on me? I never found out.

The drumming went on day and night and the stench of the corpse got worse. Each morning I dreaded having to go there again. They put the corpse on a bier made of sticks, carried it on the shoulders of four men, and started questioning it. Then it careered around the circle of spectators, stopping at various people, where one of the men would give what I was told was a sort of prophecy over them. Sometimes it stopped at me, but whatever the prophecy was it was thankfully quite unintelligible.

***

It wasn't the only time I felt frightened. Some time later I was sitting in the shade on a verandah when I thought I saw that a nearby big tree had roots just like a huge snake. Then the roots began to uncoil and rear up on end. I moved like lightning to the nearest house and told one of the women about it, who seemed very disinterested. I thought she hadn't understood so I took her by the hand to show her. "Yes," she said, "it's called the blind devil." She returned to continue pounding her rice. From the distance I looked at the 12-foot monster wriggling away and I asked her if it bit people. "Oh yes," she replied. I was baffled by her lack of concern as I knew the blind devil is an instant killer.

So I went to search for another neighbour, Fernando, to ask him why nobody was bothering but me. He laughed and explained it had been staked to the ground all day right under my nose and I hadn't noticed.

When I went closer I saw a three-forked stick that was driven into the ground, the centre fork going right through its neck. Apparently after catching the blind devil the villagers take sadistic delight in leaving it there and seeing it suffer. It was the first time I had seen such a huge snake – and I hoped I would never see one like that again, particularly one without a stake through its neck.

***

I spent the next few days, during what was supposed to be my siesta, making my room look more like home. But I didn't realize it would lead to disagreements with Val, which I handled badly. I painstakingly covered the tea chest with a length of chintz that I'd brought from England. Hand sewing was not my forte, but it looked presentable. So I then made curtains to match the two windows, which were just square holes in the wall. A hammer and nails had been in my required kit list, so it was no problem knocking the nails into the mud walls, in the hope that they would hold the string.

My two small windows each had a very ugly shutter made out of a tea chest with all its original shipping labelling painted on it. I found to my delight that the hinges were made so that the shutters could be easily lifted off, which I did. I didn't want them anyway because I much preferred the cooler air in the stifling nights. Val didn't agree. When I wasn't around she put them back on. The next night after she had gone to bed I took them off and put them outside. Later the following evening I found them back on. "It's my room isn't it?" I reasoned with my conscience.

"They are to keep the wild cats, snakes, and flying insects out," Val tried to explain.

But the shutters went off and on a few more times until the tension between us became unbearable. Then the Lord spoke to me: "Submit – isn't fellowship more important than a couple of shutters?"

"But Lord," I argued. "Have I no rights?" He answered my question then, and has had to repeat it a thousand times since. The answer was "No, you have no rights. Haven't you given them up?"

It is said that on the mission field all the dregs come to the surface. They do, and I found I had plenty. So we prayed together. I cried, the shutters stayed on, and I had peace again. However, I later had the joy of having them painted green, and they didn't bother me any more, particularly as I became more used to the stifling nights.

Another problem was the pith helmet, the miserable cork headgear we were ordered to wear all the time. Val insisted that I obeyed the rules. She had no problem with it, but I did, or at least my pride did. It looked so old-fashioned and comical. I became so good at forgetting to wear it. I even managed to leave it behind on a ferry boat one day, reasoning that an African man would appreciate it far more than I did. Thankfully, it was irreplaceable. The ticking off I got was much preferable to wearing the wretched thing.

Chapter 7

Learning Papel Was a Pig of a Job

My first task was to learn the Papel language, and every afternoon I sat among the people, asking, "What is this? How do you say such and such?"

I always had a lovely welcome and was given a rickety home-made stool. My first attempts at conversation were just a greeting.

They often roared with laughter at my attempt but were delighted when I got something right. It seemed an impossible task to learn this language.

When Val left I was joined by a young Papel Christian, Domingos Gomes, who spoke Papel and Creole fluently and understood a little Portuguese. But he could not read as he had never been to school.

He had been brought up in the Biombo region and had run away from home when he was about seventeen years old as he had leprosy. His only memory of his mum was seeing her crawling round the hut on her hands and knees with leprosy and he didn't want to end up like her. Domingos went to a clinic run by WEC where he was given medical treatment and where he became a Christian.

He moved on to Bissau, but he felt challenged to return to his people to tell them the gospel.

He knew, however, that if he left the city he was throwing away the chance of an education, and it would be very difficult to get a regular supply of the medicine he needed. Nevertheless, he decided to go home anyway. Before Domingos left the capital to return to Biombo, the Christians prayed for him and he was miraculously healed. The leprosy never reoccurred.

When he arrived back home everyone called him Boy, even his family, because he had run away and had not gone through the initiation ceremony to become a man. Every four years young boys from the age of about ten upwards are taken into the forest for a month where they are taught by the witchdoctors and put through a number of severe tests and rites. This included circumcision, performed with dirty instruments, which often led to infection and sometimes death.

It is very expensive for the families to pay for the witchdoctors, and they have to leave food every day at the edge of the forest for their sons. If a boy died in the forest the families would only find out when the doorpost of their home was splattered with blood. They believed they were forbidden by the spirits to tell anyone about their son's death because the secrecy of the ritual was all-important.

Domingos' family rejected him, saying he wasn't a true man, and they predicted he would never marry nor father any children. Eventually, Domingos won the respect of everybody, learnt to read, and became the pastor of the first church in Biombo. In 1959 he married Amelia, who had worked for Val looking after her home. Despite the family's dire predictions Domingos and Amelia went on to have eight children, all of whom lived. This was indeed a miracle in a tribe that, at about that time, had an 80 per cent infant mortality rate.

* * *

As I visited the neighbours around our little compound I was warmly welcomed into each household. I wrote down their names and then tried to learn some vocabulary. It was great fun, or at least they found it so. After some sign language they understood that I also wanted to know what the animals were called. In one household I was puzzled as several things seemed to have the same, or a very similar name, of *olanotak*. My notebook ended up with *olanotak* several times on one page.

I asked Domingos about it that evening. He looked puzzled at first, but then roared with laughter and said, "They were asking you to give them some tobacco!"

* * *

José, another Papel Christian who came from Bissau, also helped me greatly. He had a gift of telling folk-stories and I was amazed to hear him relate the Brer Rabbit stories in Papel, even though he had never heard them other than in his own language and he couldn't read. In the Papel story the fox, of course, was a hyena.

How thankful I was for Domingos and José. It would have been impossible without them. They were always so patient as I struggled to understand this complex language with its ten different groups – of what could be called "genders" or "classes" – of nouns. Each group had a different prefix that governed most of the sentence. All humans fell into the same class, animals into another group, and God and holy things such as the kapok tree and a canoe went into another. Problematically, the Holy Spirit, along with other spirits, were put into the animal class, while Jesus, of course, fell into the human class. Each of these classes had a different pronoun. This really was a headache to me, but no problem to Domingos and José.

With the two men helping me I was able to learn a little of the vocabulary and began to puzzle out the intriguing intricacies of the grammatical structure of the language. It was exciting, so different from Creole or Portuguese, so orderly, regular, and mostly consistent. The more I understood it the more I wondered how people could say that such an amazing language could have just evolved.

Unfortunately, I did not spend too much time with José, who had been converted in Bissau. But I was delighted when José produced the first Christian song with Papel words and music. It was about a wife who ran away from her husband, but he loved her so dearly, he went to look for her, forgave her, and they lived happily ever after. José changed the words to portray the love of Jesus and it became a number one hit.

Sadly, José suffered with advanced tuberculosis and died soon after I met him. I think he was probably the first Papel to arrive in Heaven!

***

The people were so patient as I struggled to learn the language, amazed that a white person would even try. One day, however, I was followed home by a crowd of boys when one was delightfully honest and said, "You've been here all this time and you can't speak our language yet." Remarks like that kept me humble.

On another occasion I was delighted when a lovely elderly Christian lady whom I had met in Bissau gave me a puppy. I called him Sonny, a little fellow with long black and white fur. As well as being cuddly and healthy he didn't have any fleas, which was most unusual in that country.

The first day Sonny arrived he disappeared, but I could hear him howling in the distance so I followed the noise to a neighbour's home. A man was sitting outside his house and I asked him if he had seen my pet. Just then a dog ran out and, greatly relieved, I picked him up and thanked the man for finding him. To my amazement he said it was his dog and his neighbour agreed. There was nothing to do but to return home again with a heavy heart. When I went to my bedroom I was astonished to find Sonny under my bed.

I immediately went back to the neighbour to show him my puppy. We stood the two side by side and they were like identical twins – same size, same markings, same face, and same fatness, except my dog had a white tip to his tail. I apologized to the other dog owner and felt very humble again.

* * *

As my language improved I became more confident and began to enjoy getting to know my neighbours. I spent one afternoon sitting outside with four ladies on low stools that were carved out of the roots of the kapok tree. We were peeling mangoes to dry in the sun. Two pigs were eagerly gobbling up the mango peel that we dropped on the ground. Conversation was lively, though I could understand only a little. I tried to ask one of the neighbours, Apili, how many babies she had had. Eventually, she answered by patting her belly and holding up both hands. Then, folding each finger down in turn and covering her breasts forlornly, she repeated it again and again. I gathered that she had had ten pregnancies so far, but not one child had survived past their second birthday. It seemed most had died shortly after birth, probably due to tetanus. How I longed to say that I could help her, but sadly I didn't have the words. I later learned that this was by no means uncommon. It was very rare to find an older woman with more than two or three children despite seeming to be forever pregnant.

Apili then picked up her sticky, messy knife and a lovely large, ready-to-eat, mango. She peeled it and cut off a slice. She handed it to the lady next to her to eat, and then cut pieces for the other two ladies, before seeming to be at a loss to know what to do next. Suddenly, she leaned over, wiped both sides of the knife on the back of one of the pigs until it was shiny clean, then cut off my piece of mango and handed it to me.

It was my first taste of Papel hospitality!

Chapter 8

Thank God for Penicillin

In those early years, mornings were usually spent learning the language, while sometimes in the afternoons Domingos and I would visit the neighbours and people in the nearby villages and in the evenings I would do language study. Domingos would share the gospel, translating for me as I told the stories in Portuguese. We were always welcomed, offered a low, carved, wobbly stool, and they would gather to listen.

I was distressed to see, in almost every home, someone very sick and often dying. Tuberculosis was rife. There was hardly a home where I didn't see someone with obvious TB. Of course, there was malaria, which affected everyone and many children died of it, plus the tropical diseases and parasitic infections, such as tapeworm, roundworm, and hookworm. Most children had huge distended bellies from malaria, malnutrition, and parasites.

The gross malnutrition of toddlers was largely due to ignorance. "He won't eat the rice – he just spits it out" was the explanation I received when I talked to a mother about weaning her toddler. The real problem was that he, like all the little ones, had been totally breastfed until two or three years old, or until the next baby was born. Suddenly, he was taken off the breast with no weaning. Then the screaming baby had boiled rice rammed down his throat, which of course he would spit out. Also, they reckoned that children shouldn't be given any grown-up food such as meat, fish, eggs, sour milk, peanut sauce, and other proteins as it would make them conceited, arrogant, and cheeky.

Another problem was the awful tropical ulcer leg wounds. When entering a little extended family compound I could often smell them. These horrible sloughing ulcers could extend right round a leg and end in death. The medicine the witchdoctors gave only speeded it up. All this suffering made them and the spirit mediums rich from the payments for animal sacrifices and their incantations. The people believed that all sickness and suffering was the result of curses put on them through malignant spirits or neglected ancestors and had to be appeased.

I began to see how their whole lives were controlled by voodoo. One year the rains came late, which called for the sacrificing of many cows. The villagers tied up the legs of cows, rowed them out to sea in canoes, and threw them overboard alive, as a sacrifice to the spirits. In the rainy season no one could begin to plough, plant, or harvest until the head shaman got the right omens. This sometimes meant a long delay so that they missed the vital rains and lost their harvest, resulting in semi-starvation.

"Dear Lord, how can I cope with all this?" I'd find myself saying as I was aware of my total inadequacy. Late one night as I walked up and down the verandah of my little house the hopelessness and loneliness overwhelmed me. "Have I made a big mistake?" I cried out. But I was reminded what God had promised me on my twenty-first birthday: "Ask of me and I shall give thee the heathen for thine inheritance" (Psalm 2:8, KJV). I knew there was no going back. As a translator I had been sent to Biombo by my field leader to turn the New Testament into Papel, but as a nurse I couldn't just stand by and watch the people suffer. "Dear Lord, you must have an answer," I prayed.

One afternoon I was in a neighbour's home where a mother was nursing a very sick toddler. He was struggling to breathe, obviously with a severe chest infection and malnutrition. I asked the mother to bring him to my house and I would give him an injection, though I wondered if he could survive the night. When she failed to arrive I took the penicillin to her house, and before she realized what I was doing I injected it into the baby's bottom. I was aware of the annoyance, or maybe the fear, of the mother and the other women.

The next day when I went back I found, to my surprise and joy, that the baby was greatly improved. The other women gathered around smiling, and no one made any objection to me giving him another injection, and then finally finishing the course. Each day as I went they happily brought out a stool for me and sat around to listen to what they called "the tasty words" as I struggled to tell them the good news about Jesus. They would try to help me out when I couldn't find the right words.

Very gradually, just one by one, women would come to me to ask for help with their sick children, so I decided to start a little clinic under the mango trees by my home. Every morning, six days a week, from 8 a.m. until lunchtime, I would take a table and chair and my basic medical equipment of penicillin and medicines, some dressings, and a few instruments, including forceps, in a jam jar containing alcohol and sit down under the mango tree and wait for patients to arrive. Word soon spread and dozens of patients came as I dealt with malaria, worms, fevers, infections, and pregnancy problems. On top of that patients came who had been attacked and wounded in a fight or bitten by a scorpion or even a snake. Once I even had to treat a man who had been mauled by a leopard and another who had been bitten by a shark. However, I wasn't allowed to treat TB, leprosy, and sleeping sickness as a nearby government clinic dealt with that. I also couldn't do much for heart conditions as I didn't have the equipment.

Miraculously, I never had to refuse anyone for lack of medicines. On one occasion a man came suffering from typhoid fever. He was the first of a few and I hadn't the appropriate antibiotic to treat typhoid as it was far too expensive. Then a woman came complaining of backache. "Will these capsules cure my backache?" she asked, showing me a large bottle of capsules of chloramphenicol, the very antibiotic I needed to treat typhoid. "Where did you get these?" I asked.

"From my son who is in the army," she answered.

I asked no more questions but offered her a bottle of aspirins in exchange. The aspirins cured her backache, and with thankfulness and prayer the capsules cured my patient's typhoid.

* * *

In one home I saw, and smelled, a lady who had a large tropical ulcer. She let me take off the leaves that covered it, revealing an extensive black mass that went almost all around her lower leg. She was feverish and ill. I suspected septicaemia and that she wouldn't have long to live. The other women stood around watching but saying nothing. I was not aware of any disapproval, but I didn't ask any questions. They were probably grateful for the dressing I put on which obscured the smell a bit. She accepted an injection of penicillin and I went back each day to repeat it. On the third day, as the women and children all gathered round to watch, I took off the dressings, revealing a delightful, red, healing area all over her leg. They all squealed and cried with astonishment, "*Koo! Koo! Koo! I guja Kristu!*" (Wow! It is God's needle!) Thank God for Alexander Fleming and penicillin!

I also had a run of very sick babies, nearly dying of measles and its complications. They were clutched from the jaws of death by this wonderful penicillin and saved from blindness with injections of vitamin A. Never a day passed without my heart being lifted up to the Lord in thanks and praise for these wonderful drugs; we will never know just how many lives have been saved through them.

* * *

That was the beginning of the fame of God's needles, and the start of us being accepted by the villagers. Perhaps they were starting to understand why we had come to their country as we talked to them about Jesus and his love for them.

Chapter 9

Happiness, but Not at the Garden of Happiness

Just four months after I had arrived in West Africa I was asked to take charge of the children's home in the suburbs of Bissau. It was called the Garden of Happiness, which, for me, was rather a misnomer.

Helen McKenzie, a Canadian missionary who was in charge, had to go home suddenly, suffering from tuberculosis and extreme exhaustion. There was no one else to care for the twenty-three babies, who were mostly children of leprous mothers. At that time the government separated those mothers from their babies. Reluctantly, I found myself with a family of twenty-three little ones, all less than five years old and all with many nursing problems, including eleven with measles and three with TB. Five of them were under a year old, and of these, two were premature babies weighing only 3 lb 2 oz each.

There was never a dull nor a spare moment. When I went to bed exhausted I took the two premature babies to sleep with me to keep them warm, and it was much easier to cope with the three-hourly feeds. If I got two hours' sleep a night I did well. Bed bugs were also a real problem. I had a blitz on them, much to the amusement of the locals. "What is all the fuss about?" they asked me. "We have them all the time. You can't get rid of them." They were probably right: I didn't. How I cried to the Lord for the strength He had promised. He gave it, though I felt like the old woman who lived in a shoe.

I had a local couple, Nana and her husband, who were supposed to do the cooking, cleaning, and washing, plus a boy to help. But they didn't. When I wanted them to do something I got a tirade of abuse. "Miss Helen never asked us to do that," they said.

I continually fought the temptation to wash floors, clean up messes, get water from the well, cook, and sort out the washing rather than face a confrontation. A dozen times a day I was tempted to sack them, but I knew I couldn't cope without them. Arguing with them was far more taxing than caring for the little ones.

The girls often dropped their wet knickers down the long-drop toilet to avoid a smacking from Nana, so I had to walk into the city to buy material and make more on the temperamental sewing machine. The boys made strategic holes in their pants that needed repairing. Thankfully, that was all the clothes they wore except on Sundays.

After just two months when I couldn't walk straight and my weight had dropped from 8 stone to 6 stone 2 lb, Kathleen Smith returned from furlough and very capably took over at the Garden of Happiness, together with a wonderful Cape Verdian Christian, Benvinda. I was sent to recuperate for a few weeks in the Bijagos Islands to be with my friend Isa Arthur, whom I had met at Bible College and who was also working for the mission as a translator. She tried to encourage me to learn the Bijagos language, but it was hopeless. I had no enthusiasm and wanted only to return to Biombo. So I spent my time there improving my Creole.

* * *

After a good rest I returned to Ondame where I had the best tonic of all, a visit from my mum and dad. What a joy that was. They coped wonderfully with the lack of amenities. Even having to put up with the tribe of cockroaches inhabiting the toilet became something of a joke. Mum did wonders cooking on a temperamental primus stove while Dad painted the miserable shutters on my windows. They sat with me under the shade of the mango tree as I treated the patients. Of course, they couldn't understand a word but they managed to communicate somehow. All the neighbours came to greet them, and they often brought presents. I had no lack of eggs and chickens then. My parents really made a hit, and as the news spread, people came from far and wide to greet them. Mum and Dad loved it.

Mum watched when I was called to a neighbour who was having her baby. She was thrilled, especially as I put the slippery wriggling baby in her hands to wrap in a towel. Then the baby's mum asked my mum what her name was. "Edith," she replied. The young girl looked disappointed until I translated it for her as Iditi. She picked up her baby girl, held her to her cheek, and said, "Now you are Iditi." That in itself was a miracle as the Papels never named their babies for some months so that the spirits wouldn't be able to get them and kill them.

* * *

I went with my parents for a wonderful two-week holiday to Varela in the cooler north of the country, where there were no mosquitoes. The luxurious comforts of the Portuguese hotel and the lazy days on the beach were a treat for me. But my parents reckoned that they enjoyed the weeks in the Biombo area even more, and it was the best holiday they had ever had.

Our field leaders, Leslie and Bessie, welcomed them in Bissau and that made a real impression, particularly on my dad, who had had a bad experience when visiting some missionaries while with the Royal Air Force in India. He remarked, "Leslie and Bessie really are genuine missionaries!"

God was answering my prayers. It was a turning point. Previously, they had been opposed to anything to do with missionary work and were suspicious of my Christian friends. Now I could look forward to my first furlough, which I knew now would be free from the tension I had previously felt at home.

Chapter 10

What a Birthday Present

The first official Papel church service was on my thirty-second birthday, 12 July 1959. Present were eleven believers, including the two evangelists, Domingos and Armando, plus myself. What a birthday present! God's promise to me on my twenty-first birthday had been fulfilled. It had all been worthwhile. We had built a small rectangular church in our village with mud walls and floor plus a straw roof. Inside were a few benches with men sitting on one side and the women on the other. As I looked around everyone there had an amazing story to tell, including these four.

✳ ✳ ✳

Paulo Mendes, a boy of about sixteen, had been following Domingos as he went from house to house talking about Jesus. He came to my house late one night and said, "I want to enter God's way."

"Why do you want to enter God's way?" I asked him.

"Because I want to have my sins forgiven and go to heaven when I die," he said. What better answer could I have had? Usually, the answer I received was "Because I want to be healed of my sickness." In such cases we advised them to keep coming to learn what it really means to enter God's way.

Paulo looked so shy and meek that I had misgivings about him standing up to the persecution that would follow. I told him of all that had happened to the other four in the village who had entered God's way and who had not been able to go through with it. However, he was quite determined, reasoning that even if they killed him he would then go to heaven. So we knelt together and he prayed his first prayer, asking Jesus to forgive his sins and come into his heart. How thrilled I was – our first convert in Biombo.

Two days later he came back very frightened. Paulo had told his family that he had "entered Christ's way" and didn't want them to make any more sacrifices for him. Also, he wanted to be excused from taking part in any of the ceremonies.

What followed was even worse than we had anticipated. The village elders gathered together and counselled him. For a boy to refuse the advice of the elderly men was unheard of. When he still stood firm his relatives gathered from all over the area and held a funeral for him. His older brother threatened Paulo that if he hadn't come out of God's way when he returned from his work in the fields he would beat him until either he gave up Christianity or was dead. His father also threatened to kill him and then commit suicide. So Paulo left the wailing, angry mob and came to us.

What could we do? We felt we couldn't shelter him in the mission. After praying, we all went back to his home together, hardly knowing what to expect. I must admit I was scared, especially as we neared the house and heard the wailing and screaming of what was supposed to be Paulo's funeral.

As we entered the compound I saw a crowd of rowdy people, but amazingly the noise suddenly stopped. Domingos called them to gather round and listen. They did. He spoke for about an hour with great power while they all stood motionless listening, hardly even heeding the mosquitoes.

Then Paulo spoke up and calmly confessed his newfound faith and told of the joy God had given him. He added, "I am so full of God that I'm laughing inside." He went on to say, "God has told me that I must respect my parents and I want to stay with you and work for you until you, too, enter God's way." This testimony was completely unprompted and seemed to be well received by the people. We came home rejoicing.

More persecution followed, and all eyes were on Paulo, waiting to see if the ruling spirit, the Iran, would kill him. I was anxious as they had probably poisoned an elderly man who had converted and who had died in suspicious circumstances.

Later, Paulo told how God had also saved him from death when he was gathering palm nuts. To cut these bunches of nuts boys must climb the tall swaying palm trees in a hoist made of plaited fibres, which go round both the tree trunk and the boy's waist. When Paulo was at the top of the tree with all his weight on the hoist he heard it splitting.

His first thought was to sing so he sang a chorus with the words: "I am not afraid to die as my name is written in the Book of Life." He threw himself against the tree trunk and inched his way down the spiky trunk without the hoist. He then took the broken hoist round the villages as a testimony to what God had done for him. Paulo went on to become a leader, not only in the Biombo region, but also of the whole country, as he was later appointed President of the Evangelical Church of Guinea-Bissau.

***

Pedrinho suffered from leprosy and had been having treatment in Bissau for years. Although the disease had been arrested and was no longer infectious the consequences were still there. The awful result of leprosy is a loss of feeling in the skin, so any wound or burn is unnoticed, resulting in infections that go untreated. Pedrinho's fingers were all just stumps, his face disfigured, and he was almost without a nose. When he joined us he was already a Christian, having been converted in Bissau. His family had made his life unbearable, not because of any risk of infection but because they thought he had the curse of the spirits on him. As a Christian he had refused to make the necessary sacrifices to appease the spirits and this put them all under a curse.

Pedrinho came regularly to the clinic to have his feet treated, which were almost toeless, having been gnawed by rats when he was asleep. His feet were a rotten, smelly mess. We did what we could with penicillin injections and dressings, and arranged a pair of shoes for him to wear in bed. This wasn't much help as then the rats only gnawed at his legs, so we found a cat for him. It was, as are all cats there, feral, but responded to some food and care and was soon sharing Pedrinho's bed. The rats never troubled him any more and his feet improved.

I found to my delight that Pedrinho spoke Creole fluently and could even read and understand a bit of Portuguese. He had a good command of Papel, his mother tongue, and was happy to help me translate the New Testament stories. He stayed in a tiny shack in our compound until we had a small, two-roomed mud house built for him by WEC visitors Ron and Mavis Rogers.

Pedrinho was so grateful for this luxury that he was happy to help in the clinic in the morning as well as work on translation with me in the evening, when we could. Then to our delight he started singing the stories we had translated into Papel. He sang them to the typical haunting, rhythmic, African Papel music, so familiar to everyone. The songs went down well in the church, and it meant that the people were unconsciously memorizing whole portions of Scripture. It proved to be the end of most of the Creole choruses with European tunes which the missionaries had translated.

I will always remember late one afternoon when I had a clinic with more than a hundred patients. It had been exhausting and finished very late. After clearing the consulting room I came out on to the verandah to find it still cluttered and dirty. It was Pedrinho's job to clear the debris and wash the floor. It was the last straw for me. I stormed round to his little house only to find him sitting on his bed reading his Portuguese Bible. In retrospect, he probably hadn't realized we had finished and that he was waiting to do his job. But I was too angry to think reasonably and told him off very sharply. Pedrinho didn't say a word. He just picked up his broom and bucket and walked over to the clinic.

That evening was the church prayer meeting. The small group of Christians gathered in my house, praying together as usual, when Pedrinho came to sit beside me. I noticed that his face was wet with tears when he began to pray, "Lord, your word says 'touch not my anointed, do my prophets no harm'. I have criticized Miss Lily; I've spoken badly of her to others. Forgive me." He sobbed – and so did I. I saw myself and it wasn't nice. All I could stutter was "I'm sorry, so sorry, Pedrinho."

Pastor Domingos got up, stood in front of us, and, putting a hand on each of us, he prayed so gently and lovingly for both of us. It was a precious moment that I will never forget.

Pedrinho always prayed fervently in our meetings for his people. Often he quoted Jeremiah 23:29: "Is not my word… like a hammer that breaks a rock in pieces?" On one occasion he got so worked up that he banged his fists on the bench with great strength, shouting, "Like a hammer, Lord, like a hammer, Lord." With a crash the fragile bench broke.

Sadly, some time later Pedrinho developed sleeping sickness and died. How we missed him. His was the first Christian funeral in Biombo. His family tried in vain to stop the Christian funeral but it was a great testimony to the many people who gathered and respectfully stood listening as Domingos preached.

* * *

Dominga was a young girl who was the third wife of a leading witchdoctor. She had heard the gospel when we went to her village three or four years previously, and she longed to "enter Christ's way". She started praying to Jesus and had taken her charms off and refused to join in the heathen ceremonies. Her witchdoctor husband said if she kept doing this he would throw her out. At planting time she and the other two wives had a patch of ground for tomatoes. While the other two made the necessary sacrifice and performed the sowing rites Dominga planted each seed "in the name of Jesus". Her faith was tried when her plants all grew weak, while the plants of the other two wives were good and strong. Of course, they didn't miss the opportunity to tell her how she was paying for her foolishness and how many other awful things would happen if she continued to offend the spirits in this way. However, Dominga stood firm and rebuked Satan. In the end her plants yielded a better crop than that of either of the other wives.

Dominga also had badly infected sores on her feet. She prayed to Jesus and she was completely healed. Then she had a vision in which God told her to go to the clinic and publicly enter His way. Previously, she had walked past our house several times but had never come in. Then one day she plucked up courage, entered, and asked how she could walk in Christ's way. She was so eager and ready and what a joy it was to have our first woman convert.

That evening Pastor Domingos accompanied Dominga back home to explain to her family what had happened. Some members agreed with the pastor; others were opposed, including the witchdoctor husband, who was very drunk. He became violent and the pastor was advised to leave. That night the husband officially divorced Dominga so she went to her father's house. He, too, was a witchdoctor and the next morning he threw her out of his house, so she came to live with and work for me. What a blessing Dominga proved to be, as she brought many Papel women to faith.

Later she fell in love with Armando, the church evangelist. However, it was decided by the national church leaders in Bissau that they shouldn't continue the relationship because a rumour was spreading throughout Biombo that our evangelists were going to the villages not to preach the gospel but to steal the local girls. Together, Armando and Dominga decided to obey and trust God for the future. A few years later they did marry and Brenda and I gave a reception for a hundred people. I also had much fun altering a pale blue dress for the bride. Eventually, the couple had six children, who all became Christians, with the eldest, Moises, becoming the principal of the country's Bible School.

***

Also there was Sabado. "Now who can this be?" I wondered, as a young emaciated woman joined our little group for our Sunday morning service. She seemed familiar, and then I remembered the last time I saw her was when I was called to her house. Sabado had been dying with what was probably some cerebral condition and was far beyond any help I could give her. They wouldn't hear of it when I suggested taking her to the hospital in Bissau. "She will die there," they said, "and we won't be allowed to bring the body back home to bury it."

I knew they were right and that it would be catastrophic as the Papel have to be buried in their own village. I pleaded with them not to make any more animal sacrifices for her but to turn to Jesus. I prayed for her but nobody was listening and Sabado was too far gone to take anything in, so I left with a heavy heart.

Imagine my joy that Sunday morning as she told us her story. Although Sabado had heard and understood what was going on she had been unable to speak and she wanted to believe. Later in a dream God told her to get up as He had healed her. She did and He had. Later, she saw the family preparing to sacrifice a goat in thanksgiving for her healing. "No!" Sabado said. "It is Jesus who has healed me and I'm going to His house to enter His way." Her mother beat her and refused to give her food, saying that she was bringing the curse of the spirits on the whole family, but she stood firm.

Sabado explained to us how she had been possessed by a spirit who had made her walk through fire and sometimes in the ceremonial dancing she had leapt on to the rooftops and danced in a trance. After finishing telling her story Sabado was delivered of the spirit and became a Christian. What a morning service! What a birthday present!

Chapter 11

A Difficult Homecoming and the Question of Marriage

It was 1962, and with a mixture of emotions I prepared to leave Ondame to go home to Liverpool for the first time in nearly six years. What was I leaving behind as I went on my first furlough? I looked back at all that had – and had not – been achieved.

What progress had I made in the language work in five years? Very little really, compared with what a Wycliffe worker would achieve. Yes, the language had been reduced to writing with a tentative alphabet produced, and I had enjoyed discovering the complex and consistent grammatical structure. Thanks to God's gift of Domingos with his fluency in Papel and Creole we had the first translation of Mark's Gospel duplicated. It was a beginning, but oh so little.

In the church there was just a little group of around eleven sincere and loving believers. In the village my neighbours were friendly and warm people who totally accepted me, but they were still unmoved by the good news we had tried to tell them about the gospel.

One afternoon I stood with Domingos, Pedrinho, and Armando on a hillside, looking down on the scene before us. We had just come away from the funeral there. I was deeply disturbed as I thought of the task that lay before us. There was a swarming, screaming mass of people below in a clearing where the grotesque monstrous body of the village chief lady witchdoctor lay. The corpse was wrapped, as is their custom, in layer upon layer of cloths, until the body with its extended limbs was twice or three times its normal size. She had died ten days ago, and in spite of all the wrappings, the smell was foul. We listened to the monotonous rhythm of the drums and the eerie wailing and chanting. We watched the frenzied dancing and caught, even at a distance, the stench of the corpse. I had been sickened to see the reeling drunkenness of the witchdoctors and the glazed eyes of the little drummer boys as they were given the potent native "fire-water" to drink. Then Armando voiced all our thoughts when he said, "We need a revival." Pedrinho with his invincible faith added, "It's got to be. It will be."

Although the church grew slowly, the clinic certainly didn't. The medical work, simple though it was, moved rapidly, with up to a hundred people coming each day, all wanting "the needle".

"Give me God's needle" was the typical request of most of the patients.

"What for?" I would ask.

"For my body," many replied.

"What part of your body?" I would ask.

"All of it," they said.

Of course. Why did I ask?

✴ ✴ ✴

Almost every person in the Biombo area suffered from something, whether it was malaria, TB, tropical ulcers, worms, or a mixture of infections. Many were beyond my help and the meagre medical facilities I had. I would try to persuade the very ill patients to go to the hospital in Bissau, but I knew they only went away disgruntled and consulted a witchdoctor.

Sometimes they would bring a dying toddler, with its abdomen horribly lacerated by the witchdoctor, who had bled the child to bring out the evil spirit. They would draw out about a third of a pint of blood with a very hot coconut shell. At least I could treat the malaria and try to combat the gross anaemia that the little ones had. People came to me with huge stinking ulcers treated by the witchdoctors with cow dung. There were children suffering badly from malnutrition and adults dying with TB, whom the spirit mediums had forbidden to eat any food other than unsalted rice. Many babies died in the first few weeks of life through tetanus. They were infected at birth as they were delivered on a dirt floor in the dark room where the cows and goats slept at night. No official records were kept, but I would estimate that up to 30 per cent of babies born died of tetanus within two weeks of birth.

All sicknesses and calamities were accredited directly or indirectly to the ruling spirit, the Iran, who had to be continually appeased with animal sacrifices. Tetanus was from an evil spirit of a monkey or a cat. It was always fatal, in spite of the costly sacrifices the parents made. These sacrifices kept the witchdoctors and spirit mediums well fed, but their patients in deep poverty.

The medical needs had taken so much of my time. I was anxious because the medical work had grown considerably beyond my ability to cope without help. It was very low-key and lacked the essential equipment and skills that were so needed.

I was also worried because a few of my senior colleagues in Bissau disapproved of it. "Lily, you shouldn't be doing all this," someone said at our mission conference. "Our task is to preach the gospel."

"The medical needs of the people should be the government's responsibility," someone else said. "The translation of the New Testament should be your priority and it isn't, is it?"

They were right, but were they totally right? Wasn't "God's needle" or penicillin the way we could show our Heavenly Father's love for the people and so earn the right to tell them about Jesus and translate the New Testament into their language? Here I was going home, and leaving people I had grown to love, knowing that there would be many unnecessary deaths in the year I would be away. There was no other missionary nurse available to help them.

Could the answer be Brenda Couche, a good friend whom I met through the Nurses' Christian Fellowship, and whom I then worked with at St Paul's Eye Hospital in

Lily Gaynor, seated far right, aged 22, and Isa Arthur, seated far left, when they attended the WEC prayer meeting hosted by Ted and Ethel Bushell while Lily was training to be a midwife.

The main road from Biombo to the capital of Guinea-Bissau.

Brenda Couche, WEC missionary and Lily's co-worker.

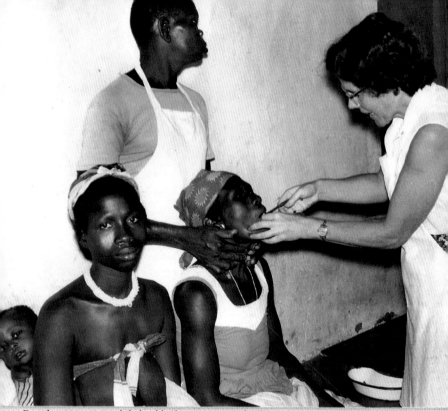

Brenda extracts a tooth helped by her assistant Pedrinho.

The Portuguese ladies, Mena Almeida (left) and Olinda Pedroso (far right), who took over the Biombo clinic when Brenda Couche (second left) and Lily Gaynor retired.

Domingos, the first pastor of the Biombo church.

WEC missionaries Brenda Couche (left) and Lily Gaynor.

Lily Gaynor helps dub the Jesus film into Papel.

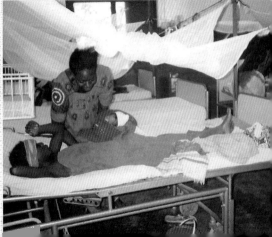

Nurse Loida Patrao who ran the Biombo clinic for a while after Lily and Brenda retired to England.

Lily's parents, John and Edith Gaynor, visited Lily in Portugal at Christmas 1956.

A rare picture of an idol in a sacred forest.

The mud huts in Biombo with the witchdoctor's tiny consulting hut on the right.

The Biombo maternity unit.

One of the many shrines where sacrifices are made.

A Papel spirit medium's consulting room.

Lily, aged 13, with her long hair which her grandmother said was the reason Lily was not working hard enough at school.

Lily, aged 32, on the right, with WEC mission team leaders Bessie and Leslie Brierley in 1959.

A feared witchdoctor.

Brenda Couche with children from the Garden of Happiness.

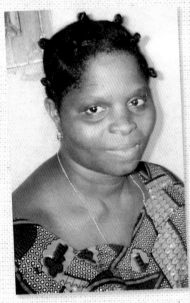
Midwife Ana Rita.

Lily Gaynor and a local Christian, Armando Pereira, in the Ondame compound.

Midwife Celeste who married Bilopat.

Ursula Pasut (right), who keyed
the New Testament into Papel.

Local Christians Tito and Ana.

Pastor Quintino, who was
one of the Bible translators.

The upgraded clinic in Biombo.

Having a wash Biombo-style at the well.

The huge sacred kapok tree.

Evangelism in one of the Biombo villages.

WEC missionary Betty Dutch.

Lily Gaynor.

Christian ladies in Biombo.

Liverpool? She arrived just before Christmas, 1961, on the same boat that I had come on. It was with great joy that I went to Bissau to welcome her. I went on board and what a reunion it was. I felt encouraged that she would possibly be coming to join us when I returned from furlough.

But as the staff situation in Bissau was acute and there was nobody who could take charge of the babies in the Garden of Happiness, Brenda was sent there. What a challenge to have to cope with twenty-three babies and children who spoke only Creole while Brenda spoke only Portuguese. My heart ached for her.

What about when I returned? Would it be to Biombo to continue work on the New Testament? I hoped so. But then how could I refuse to treat these needy people who trusted and relied on me? Would Brenda be allowed to join me there?

Physically I was quite low, much thinner and exhausted, but spiritually a lot wiser about my shortcomings as I set off for Liverpool. Still I was very aware that Jesus had been with me all the way and had fulfilled His promises during my first six years abroad.

* * *

I had never heard of culture shock before, but it soon hit me as I arrived in Liverpool. Things had changed. I didn't fit in. I was puzzled and sometimes shocked to see how people dressed. The abundance of food in the new, strange supermarkets was overwhelming and made me somewhat sad to see it. The language and innuendos on the TV were disturbing. It wasn't long after I got hooked on watching

TV that I began to see that so often wrong was acceptable and right was ridiculed.

How could I pray "lead me not into temptation" and then sit and watch some of the programmes? Why was there no enthusiasm in church services? Why did it seem that people were reluctant to talk about Jesus? Why were there long silences in the prayer meetings? This grieved me so much that I didn't know what to do. I would end a long silence several times by praying aloud until someone told me I was monopolizing the prayer meeting. To sit and join the silence was painful but, as so often happened, I would succumb to my unhealthy desire to be liked and so conform.

I had to adapt, but it wasn't easy at first. I remembered a maxim of our principal in Bible College – "Others may, you may not!" – and that helped. I was wrong, of course, in my judgmental attitude about other Christians. It was just another culture! The Lord, as always, was patient with me and soon I realized that I was accepted and loved in the church that had supported me as best they could for the past six years. The pedestal they put me on was disturbing. "Come and meet our missionary!" someone would say, as if I was some special saintly exhibit. I cringed, often thinking, "if only they knew…" I looked forward to getting back to the field where I would be cut down to size again.

One of the big trials to a career missionary is the frequent tearing up of roots. A year at home, happy though I was, was too long. I had settled back into my comfort zone. Dad had given me a car so I enjoyed being able to speak at meetings and meet so many lovely prayer supporters. When Dad sold the car at the end of the year he said to the buyer, "It was my daughter's; she only used it to go to church." This perhaps gave the wrong impression, as I was not attending only one local church but churches all over the country.

The memories of the problems and heartaches on the field loomed large, and I felt I couldn't face it again. Yet strangely my heart longed to go back. But I was in my mid-thirties and the hormones were still active. Was there a possibility of marriage? Yes, vaguely! I was interested in someone and thought he was interested in me. Could this be God's will for me now? Could I follow it up? If so, I knew there would be no possibility of returning to West Africa. But I knew deep down that marriage wasn't really God's will for me, so I dismissed that thought. There was no turning back. "Hadn't I promised to be His and His only for ever? Hadn't I sacrificed my rights?" I thought to myself as I packed to return to the mission field.

Chapter 12

Brenda Helped Me Live like a Queen

What a thrill – my first ever flight! It was 1963 as we flew in low over the swampy terrain of the country at high tide. The sea swept in like a spider's web through the thick green forest land. Here and there I could pick out the tiny villages, surrounded by water, and the tortuous tracks leading to the small towns. Then I saw Bissau airport and, joy of joys, the group of missionaries and Africans waving furiously. I was home. Brenda was there with Domingos and several others. They had even brought my dog, Onejo (Sonny's successor), which is Papel for "blessed", to welcome me. I choked back my thanks to Jesus through tears of joy as we hugged one another.

I was soon on the bumpy road to Biombo again. As we neared our village of Ondame people came running out on to the road, crying, "*Mislili bili, U bili, u bili*" ("Miss Lily, you've come back") , so we stopped to greet them.

When we drew into our compound I was surrounded and overwhelmed by the welcome and the gifts of eggs and a chicken. I was delighted to hear that Brenda would be joining me in Ondame and was eager to prepare for her arrival. Brenda's middle-class background had been so different from mine. She had gone to a good boarding school and had trained at one of the top London hospitals. How would she react to the primitive situation in West Africa? How would the friendship stand up to the pressures and inadequacies? My experiences with Val had made me realize how careless I was of another's feelings and needs.

My worries were groundless. One word described Brenda: "graciousness". I met her as she got off the rickety old bus that made the daily eight-hour and 40-mile journey from Bissau to Biombo. It had wooden seats with no cushions and just an iron bar as a back rest, but she had coped well with all the bumps and rattles.

She quickly recovered from the journey after a cup of tea and was delighted to see our two little square, thatched, cottage-like houses. She had expected to be living in a round mud hut in the centre of a crowded village. Not so! Though the village was all around us it was not the squalid jumble of dwellings like on the outskirts of Bissau. Each extended family had a group of four or five round houses which were, at that time, built in a circle and joined together by their roofs. It was fascinating, but sadly square houses became more fashionable in later years. The family dwellings were surrounded by small fields and here and there huge trees and bushes. Even in the dry season it was refreshing and beautiful, but in the rainy season it was exquisitely African, mosquitoes and all!

What a wonderful difference Brenda's coming made to me. We enjoyed rearranging the two houses so that the bigger one could become a medical centre with one room as the clinic and the other two rooms as the "maternity" section. It was a thousand times better than the table and chair under the mango trees. The number of patients soared and we soon had up to 150 coming most days. We bought a bed and mattress, drew up a design for a dressing table-cum-desk, and had a table and chairs made by a carpenter in Bissau from lovely African mahogany – and all for about £12. When Brenda arrived someone said she talked like the Queen. Now she lived like one – and so did I.

* * *

Brenda settled in quickly, adjusted to our diet of mainly rice and fish, and was soon experimenting in the kitchen, producing more interesting meals. Her Portuguese was better than mine because she talked with people more, and likewise her Creole, which she quickly picked up. But I never managed to persuade her to learn Papel. Brenda was practical; she rarely read a book but just loved to be with people. She was also artistic and enjoyed making a series of six reading primers with simple illustrations. Brenda then arranged reading classes with a few of our local children and the new believers. We duplicated the pages and made the first reading books in Papel. Later we produced little health books with my typewriter and the mission duplicator. It was fun.

Then we had the joy of a visit from our good friend, Betty Dutch, who had supported us for many years. She fitted in so well, relieving us of the household duties and producing lovely and unexpected meals, in spite of a primus stove that needed almost continual pumping. Betty was such a blessing, not just then but all through the years that followed. She prayed for us continually and would move heaven and earth to get us anything we needed. Her parcel was wrapped in prayer and always arrived safely.

Sometime later, Pat Connelly, another dear friend of ours, visited us. She was a nurse/midwife, much more up to date than Brenda and me. Pat was a great help and taught us a lot. She loved it and after her three months were up she didn't want to go home. We didn't want her to go either.

Chapter 13

Food Problems
as War Erupts

Although Portugal had claimed Portuguese Guinea since 1446, it didn't become one of their overseas provinces until 1952. Four years later, in 1956, Amilcar Cabral and Rafael Barbosa founded the African Party for the Independence of Guinea and Cape Verde (PAIGC) to try to oust the colonialists.

After a strike by dock workers in Bissau on 3 August 1959 was put down violently with the loss of fifty lives in what became known as the Pijiguiti Massacre, the rebels moved their headquarters to Conakry in neighbouring Guinea where they continued the armed struggle. War broke out in January 1963 when the PAIGC guerrillas attacked the Portuguese garrison in Tite, south of Bissau. They received support from Senegal, Guinea, Cuba, and the Soviet Union, and the fighting soon spread to the eastern and northern parts of the country. In a war later called "Portugal's Vietnam", the PAIGC soon succeeded in controlling two-thirds of the country, reducing Portuguese military and administrative command to a relatively small area. As I was living in the west of the country and travelling to the capital once a month for groceries, I was well away from the fighting but not unaffected.

In a letter home on 29 April 1963, I wrote:

> We've got a war on and the whole of the south of the country is closed to us now and the believers are scattered. We know of six of our leading Christians who have been killed – and who knows how many more. It isn't a religious persecution, though sometimes an antagonist to the gospel will take the opportunity to get vengeance on a Christian. Refugees are pouring into the capital, Bissau, where there is no work and very little food.
>
> Portuguese planes are patrolling all the time. It means that no one dares work in the fields so no rice planting is being done, which means there will be a bad famine this year. Of course, the Portuguese military strength is too much for the rebels though they are being supplied with arms. But one wonders how long this war can go on or what will happen in the rainy season. The PAIGC will have a definite advantage then when the roads are cut off to armoured cars. However, I think the city of Bissau is strongly guarded and I should add almost impregnable to the rebels.

Life was difficult for the locals and precarious for the missionaries who had to keep well out of the politics. In another letter home I wrote:

Our position as missionaries is delicate. The Portuguese have kept the whole situation a tight secret. Judging by the complete silence from even African broadcasting stations on the subject it seems as though they have been successful in keeping their troubles to themselves.

All our movements are suspect now and we are watched continually, though there has been no actual restriction to the preaching of the gospel. The Portuguese plain-clothed policemen stand outside our church at each service listening to all that is said through the open window so we have got to be very careful that we make no mention of anything that sounds even vaguely political.

It is surprising how many passages of Scripture could be interpreted politically. Sometimes it seems there's hardly anything left to preach about.

Actually there is little to fear for the white missionary. If things got too hot we would probably be asked to leave and it is very unlikely we would be attacked or maltreated by either side. It is the local Christians who need our prayers for whom there is no way of escape. When the trouble reaches their area they must align themselves with one side or the other and they are between two fires. There is no possibility of a plane or boat to England for them.

We are an embarrassment to the Portuguese as we are a likely source of any leaks or information. Consequently, letters in and out of the country are carefully read. Can you all make sure that there is nothing even vaguely political and do not refer to politics, wars, persecution, or the death of Christians in letters to me.

***

As I expected life became very difficult from 1963 onwards and for six months food was a huge problem. After partial independence there was still very little in the shops, only tins of Russian meat that were eight years old, plus some totally useless gifts of aid that included toothpicks, bubblegum, and antifreeze – ironic when temperatures were tropical all the year round.

When France sent a planeload of food to help the people it was turned away as the new government did not want to accept help from the West, only from the Communists. We lived on bananas and food parcels sent from the UK. However, we didn't lose a single food parcel, probably because both sides respected us and knew we had come to help the ordinary people.

Many local people survived on mangrove pods, which had to be boiled seven times because they contained so much salt. However, one day our food did run out. "Miss Brenda, Miss Lily, come and look at this," said Quinta, our helper who cooked the midday meal for us. She led us to the store room and took off the lid of the tank where the rice was stored. Then, looking up and holding up her hands, Quinta said, "Lord Jesus, just look at this – rice, rice, Lord. Please send us rice now."

As Brenda and I looked we were dismayed to see just a sprinkling of food in the bottom of the tank. We needed rice for our staff, but we also desperately had to have milk, sugar, oil, and rice to feed the pitiful, starving children who came to us each day. What could we do? The next morning I set out early to make the tortuous journey to Bissau. I was determined to get to see someone in authority who could help us. We knew that food came in from relief organizations from Holland, Sweden, and America. There was one called Food for the World, so I went to their office in Bissau and asked to see the boss. He wasn't in; he had gone to see a government minister. I ignored the usual "Come back tomorrow" and sat and waited for him.

After an hour or more he stormed into his office, threw his papers on his desk, and sat down. He saw me and barked "What do **YOU** want?" I told him who I was and explained our situation. My heart sank as he said, "All the food we get goes to the army. You can go. I'll look into it." End of interview.

I went home that day thinking, "Well, our hope isn't in man; it is only in you, Lord." Two days later, in the early hours of the morning, we were awakened by the noise of a huge lorry coming up our drive. Never before had such a vehicle come to us. We went out to investigate and saw two men unloading sacks and sacks of rice, dried milk, and sugar together with several gallon cans of edible oil. What a surprise and what a joy as we quickly put them in the garage. They had come at night and returned immediately to avoid the checkpoints. But that was also a blessing. If they had come during the day it would have been chaotic, with mobs of pleading people running after the lorry. Amazingly, none of our neighbours heard it. Our feeding programme continued and many children's lives were saved.

After that the food situation improved as aid arrived. In 1968 a new Portuguese governor to Bissau, General Antonio de Spinola, introduced a series of civil and military reforms, first to contain the PAIGC and then to push them back. For the next four years the general tried to win the hearts and minds of the local people by building new schools, a hospital, and an improved telecommunications and road network. Until then Portuguese armed forces were made up of white officers and commissioned soldiers and overseas soldiers from other African countries. The general brought local Guinea Africans into the army and set up special commando, marine, and other units who went on the offensive.

On 22 November 1970, the Portuguese amphibious assault troop attempted to overthrow Ahmed Sekou Toure, the leader of the neighbouring Republic of Guinea and staunch PAIGC ally in a daring raid on Conakry. Although the attempted *coup d'état* failed the PAIGC leader Amilcar Cabral was assassinated three years later in January 1973.

But all this did was give the PAIGC more support, with countries such as Nigeria and Algeria offering help and the Soviet Union sending warships in a show of force to deter Portuguese troops from attacking Guinea again. When the Carnation Revolution, a left-wing military movement, broke out in Portugal on 25 April 1974, it was the end of the Portuguese dictatorship of Estado Novo.

The new regime quickly ordered a ceasefire and began negotiating with leaders of the PAIGC.

Portugal granted the country full independence on 10 September 1974, after eleven and a half years of armed conflict. They officially recognized the new government controlled by the PAIGC and headed by Luis Cabral, half-brother of the assassinated Amilcar Cabral, as Portuguese Guinea became officially Guinea-Bissau.

Chapter 14

"Your labour is not in vain in the Lord"

1 Corinthians 15:58

With Brenda's arrival and the extended new clinic with the two maternity rooms, it meant that we could concentrate on general medical work on Mondays, Wednesdays, and Fridays, and pre- and post-natal care on Tuesdays and Thursdays, plus visits to the villages in the afternoons. Slowly, as word spread, women began to come to us and a small maternity unit was born at the clinic, which soon averaged forty deliveries a month.

Sometimes a mother would start out to come to us when her labour had gone on too long, or she became worried. Sometimes a witchdoctor would do his divination and then send the mother to us. Ironically, he would then get a chicken or a goat in payment for his advice! Occasionally, a mother would deliver on the way to us. What a mess that was. The baby was always coated in mud and dirt and it took several washes in warm water and disinfectant as we scraped off the mud, grass, and weeds. Once in a while relatives would object to the warm-water washing, saying that it had to be cold water or the child would never get married. There was no explanation and I never found out why they said that. Gradually, however, most mothers accepted our strange methods, which were undoubtedly preferable to the horrific and barbaric deliveries performed by the witchdoctors and the old women "birth-attendants".

The mothers were always happy to have us pray to Jesus for a safe delivery, and thanked Him afterwards. How we shared their joy. However, we had quite a battle in getting the mother to go home afterwards. "Please let me stay here till the cord comes off," a mother would plead. "The evil eye will get the baby and kill him if I leave Christ's house while the umbilical cord is still on." I never did get to the bottom of that reasoning, but evidently there was protection under our roof.

The frequent call-outs into the villages sometimes meant a long walk or bike ride, and always meant a complication, or we had been summoned too late. For about twelve years until the mid-1970s we had no transport of our own other than a bike or moped. There was no possibility of a telephone. The nearest hospital was 40 miles away, and the few patients whom we persuaded to go there were often too far gone, and died on the ward.

Some of the conditions we faced were horrific, but somehow we got used to it. The dramas and emergencies were all in a day's work – or, more often, a night's work. Where the midwife's textbook said "Call for medical aid", Brenda would visit me or I would go to Brenda and we would both call on the Lord. Sometimes He gave us a real miracle, far beyond our training or abilities. Other times He didn't, but we never had a maternal death on our hands, which was a miracle in itself. It was a joy to hear remarks from villagers like "Christ is powerful. Go to Christ's house and your baby will live. Babies born on Christ's bed don't die." And there were some amazing stories of babies surviving against all odds.

* * *

Apili, one of my neighbours whom I had first met while I was learning the language and who wiped her knife on a pig before cutting me a piece of mango, came to see me rather sheepishly one morning. "*Mislili nji bili*" ("Miss Lily, I've come"), she proclaimed. I was surprised and greeted her enthusiastically. For weeks I had been trying to persuade her to let us deliver what was probably her eleventh baby, as none of her previous babies had lived beyond their second birthday – though I don't think anybody in the Biombo area knew the date of a birthday, and few children knew their ages. Apili had come alone, which was strange, and she was obviously fearful. Probably none of the other women had agreed to her coming, but of course we were delighted.

We quickly set everything up, excited to have the opportunity to do things professionally and also to give Quinta, our helper, a practical lesson. But then we began to make a series of mistakes. Apili was more than hesitant about the soap and water wash, and was very reluctant to get on the bed, but I insisted. Thankfully, when we examined her, it promised to be a normal delivery. The foetus was in the right position and the heartbeat was good.

However, Apili became more and more agitated. We were ignorantly doing all the wrong things, so she thought, and scaring her to death. "You are doing fine, Apili," I tried to reassure her, but with little success. My back was turned for a minute when she jumped off the bed and ran home, at a surprising speed for a woman in the final stage of labour.

The baby was delivered stillborn on the dirt floor of her house. The cord had been wrapped around the neck and strangled the baby. This is a common problem that any midwife or doctor could have rectified, had they been there. How sad we were. We realized that our efforts to do everything efficiently had proved disastrous.

A year later, after much persuasion, Apili turned up again to be delivered. This time we dispensed with all the preliminaries, laid a sheet on the floor of the delivery room, and just let her get on with it. The sheet, of course, was a compromise which she accepted, relieved that she didn't have to get on to the bed. She just stooped on the sheet in the way she was accustomed to doing. Again the cord was short and tightly wound around the baby's neck. Had she delivered this baby at home it too would have been stillborn. She now had a lovely baby girl, her only child, who grew up to be a fine Christian lady and a wonderful help to her mother. The news of Apili's safe delivery soon spread all around the neighbourhood

✳ ✳ ✳

"Senhora, come, the baby has only half come out" was all too often the despairing cry of a husband, as he rushed to us. During these times I would find myself praying, "Dear Lord, another breech with extended arms. Please let me get there in time."

We would invariably find the totally exhausted mother sitting on the three stones that held the cauldron when cooking rice. For two or three days, she had suffered unmentionable, torturous efforts to pull or push the baby out. Usually the baby was already dead, the mother shocked and traumatized. Within minutes I would have the baby out – it really is easy when you know how! Then there would be cries of relief and sheer admiration from the spectators: "Coo! Coo! It is Christ! Christ is powerful."

I would go home, sad for the intense suffering of the mother and loss of her baby, but thankful that her life was saved. Without us the mother would have died after several more days of agony and torture, like so many others in the same situation. I wondered why there were so many breech deliveries with extended arms, and if there would ever be a breakthrough. Would we ever be able to have an efficient midwifery unit with ante-natal clinics and be able to teach these women?

***

"Oh! Another one born on the way," I sighed, as a worried-looking woman burst into the clinic, saying, "Please come, Miss Lily! My daughter has had her baby in the peanut field." I picked up my case and left right away, walking with her across the road into the field. I was thankful it wasn't a long way off.

I found the mother looking exhausted sitting among the plants. The baby, still attached to the placenta, was curled up in a large gourd. He was covered in mud and leaves. I separated the placenta there and then and wrapped the baby in a towel. We made our way, stumbling over the peanut plants, to the maternity unit. Her mother and another lady were half-carrying and half-walking her, while I carried the baby. We helped her on to the examination couch. I thought she looked rather shocked. I felt her abdomen to see if the uterus had contracted normally, but was amazed that I couldn't feel anything at all. Then to my horror I saw the uterus lying inside-out between her knees. It was covered with dirt and leaves. The two women had probably been pulling furiously at the cord and pulled the whole uterus out. It was a miracle she hadn't bled to death.

I called Brenda. We had never had a case like this before. Obviously, the first thing was to treat the mother for shock, sedate her, and give an intravenous antibiotic. Then we had to heat water, wash, and as far as possible clean it all up. They had refused to consider going to the hospital in the city. The mother's husband was away on a journey and she couldn't go without his permission. "He wouldn't give it anyway," they said.

So the next thing was to try to push the uterus back into place. "Please Lord, I need supernatural wisdom," I said. Slowly and gradually I eased it back into place, bit by bit, until I was happy that it felt normal. I inserted a ring to secure it until we could contact the husband and persuade him to take her to the hospital to have the necessary surgery. It was frustrating that the husband never turned up, but somehow the mother was well and apparently normal when she returned to clinic sometime later to have the baby vaccinated. I don't know whether the mother had any other babies after that.

✳ ✳ ✳

"Miss Lily, my baby is dead!" cried one of the women from the family next door, as she threw herself at my feet in floods of tears. An hour previously I had treated the baby for a very high fever and had given the appropriate anti-malarial treatment. I took her back home and the baby was indeed dead. It was such a distressing situation and I wondered whether the family would blame the injection, but thankfully they didn't. Her only other child, a very sickly, weak toddler, was suffering from gross malnutrition, so I had been giving him egg in milk every day to try to build him up and to stop him from going the way of so many other toddlers. He survived and she was so grateful.

The same day that our neighbour's baby died I had been asked to go to a woman who had been, so they said, in labour for twelve hours. They failed to say she had been bleeding for two days. I found her, lying on the ground in a pool of blood, deathly white, semi-conscious, and I could just feel a faint pulse. There was nothing I could do. A forceps delivery was impossible in this case. She needed blood and an immediate Caesarean section. I wrote a note and offered my bike for someone to go to the administrative centre 20 miles away, where there was a phone, to call for an ambulance. My pleadings, threats, and warnings were all of no avail. No way would they allow her to go to the hospital.

What could I do? I felt angry with them and frustrated. Too angry, I think, to pray. With the steady, unstoppable trickle of blood she could last only a few hours. The hopelessness of it all overwhelmed me. "Well," I thought when I calmed down, "it's good that they didn't agree to her going to the hospital; she couldn't possibly have survived the journey, and I may have got the blame."

So I sat silently with them and waited for death. God in his love and mercy overlooked my lack of faith and gave a wonderful miracle. She delivered a stillborn baby about an hour later, and then the torn placenta was delivered and so the bleeding stopped, but I could feel no pulse. I thought the mother had died. But no, she had survived. There was no explanation for it. It was one of the many miracles that God gave us that began to open the door in Biombo to the gospel.

* * *

"Lily, there is something wrong here," Brenda called out. I joined her in the labour ward thinking, "It's a good job nobody here speaks English." Indeed, there was something wrong. The woman had been quite a long time in labour and now she had delivered the baby's head, but Brenda was struggling to get the shoulders and arms down. Eventually she did, but there it stuck, the baby half out. The blueness of the baby's face was ominous, but there was still a faint heartbeat. "The cord is trapped," Brenda said as she tried to ease it free, but without success. The tiny bit of umbilical cord that was showing was flat, white, and extremely taut. "I'll have to clamp and cut it if I can," Brenda added. But then, as she tried to get the clamping forceps around the cord, it suddenly snapped, shooting back out of reach! We gasped with horror as the baby rapidly delivered followed by a frightening and continuous flow of blood.

"Can you get the end of the cord?" I asked, as I held the baby, relieved that he was breathing and his heartbeat was improving – but my heart was beating faster. The blood continued to flow rapidly and uncontrollably, saturating the sheet.

"No, the cord has gone up," she answered. "I can't get it."

"Then go in and try to get it," I said, my alarm mounting, and trying to keep any panic out of my voice.

"With no anaesthetic!" Brenda gasped. It wasn't a question. She knew full well the implications.

"We'll lose her if you don't," I replied. We both knew that unless we had a miracle we would lose her anyway.

"Lord, please!" Brenda whispered as she faced the challenge. Then, with the blood running down her arm and off her elbow, she exclaimed, "I've got the end of the cord... I think... No... Yes... But it is too slippery to hold!"

I thrust the long-handled clamp into her left hand, with which she managed, eventually, to clamp the stump of cord, and the bleeding slowed to a trickle. "Thank you, Lord, but we aren't out of the woods yet," Brenda prayed. I gave the injection to make the uterus contract and within a couple of minutes Brenda was able to remove the placenta manually and the bleeding stopped.

What a relief! The poor mother was, as we expected, quite shocked, but she soon revived after we had cleaned up the mess and warmed her up with a hot water bottle and a drink. Both mother and baby recovered and did well. The umbilical cord was only 5 inches long. Never, in all the many deliveries we have had through the years, have we experienced another incident of such a short cord, and we've never known a cord to snap. It was a miracle! Had she delivered at home in the village she would have died. Of course, today, in a hospital in the West the short umbilical cord would have been diagnosed early and a Caesarean section performed. My midwifery tutor used to say that the most dangerous journey we make in all our life is the journey down the birth canal. I think she was right.

***

That same day a four-day-old baby, from the house over the road, died of tetanus. Even though the mother lived so close she had failed to come to the clinic, but had delivered on the dirt floor in the room where the pigs and goats were brought in at night. In the animal droppings and darkness tetanus germs thrived. We longed to be able to run a vaccination programme for the pregnant women to stop this plague of tetanus. We reckoned that about one in four babies died of neonatal tetanus. It could so easily be prevented. But how could we get the injections, which need to be transported in cold storage and then kept in a fridge? Without electricity it was just a dream.

However, some years later we did manage to buy a paraffin fridge, and UNICEF provided the injections, not only for tetanus but also for the five necessary vaccinations for the babies. So again God answered prayer and a successful vaccination programme was begun for the whole area.

As this programme developed we found that mothers often failed to bring their babies for the second and subsequent injections. Brenda knitted some vests which we gave to the newborn babies when they had their first TB vaccination, and promised a bigger vest when they brought the baby for the fifth vaccination at five months old. This worked wonders, so much so that it was later reported on the radio that our clinic had the best vaccination figures in the whole country. It was all due to the knitting groups and individuals in Merseyside who kept us supplied with vests. Eventually, deaths from neonatal tetanus became very rare, and the number of fatalities for measles epidemics was much lower.

✳ ✳ ✳

Some of the babies who were stillborn could have been delivered alive by vacuum extraction had we had the instrument. How we longed for this expensive equipment. It would cost up to £200, which was far beyond our budget at that time. We prayed about it. Was it possible? If we had one could we learn to use it? Would it work without electricity? The Lord seemed to say, "Yes, what do you want? Ask and it shall be given to you."

On my next home leave I arranged to spend a week in a hospital in Warwick where I could learn how to use the machine. I was disappointed that they didn't have a single case when they needed the machine while I was there, but a female obstetrician took an interest in me and taught me a lot. She had been a missionary in India. On my last day there she said, "I have a new ventouse vacuum extractor still in the box. I bought it to take to India but I couldn't go back. If you haven't got one, would you like it?"

I could hardly believe my ears! "Oh thank you," I stammered through tears of joy. "Yes, I would love to buy it from you," I said, reckoning that the Lord had led me this far so he would give me whatever she asked.

"No," she said, "I am giving it to you."

What a miracle! Jesus had led me to the very hospital in England where a lovely child of His had a hand-operated vacuum extractor to give to me. They are very rarely used now in hospitals in England. Who else in the world would have a new one to give away? Who else but God could have arranged to have me there to meet her at just the right time?

It proved to be a Godsend in every sense of the word. Many babies were saved through this precious gift, and possibly even the lives of mothers. We used it often, and rarely needed to use the obstetric forceps again. Also the trauma of transferring a woman to Bissau for a Caesarean section, with all its dangers, was avoided in many instances.

***

One morning Brenda skipped breakfast. She had been vomiting during the night and looked awful. When I took her temperature it was 40 degrees Celsius. I insisted that she didn't come to the clinic, gave her the usual malaria treatment, and left her in bed.

The clinic that morning was hectic, with many patients waiting. Two toddlers were brought in, both convulsing, with extremely high temperatures and desperately ill. At the same time our trainee midwife, Ana Rita, asked me to see a mother in the maternity who had obstructed labour and needed help.

"I'll come as soon as I can," I said, "when I've got these two toddlers a bit cooler and stable." About an hour later I rushed to the maternity, anxiously worrying and guilty because of the delay. There, to my amazement, I found the mother sleeping peacefully with her baby all wrapped up snugly beside her, while Ana was washing the ventouse vacuum extractor.

"You didn't do it, did you?" I gasped.

"No," she said, "go and see Miss Brenda." Sure enough, Brenda was back in bed and in spite of her temperature, which was still very high, she smiled, pretended to look guilty, and said, "Thank God for the ventouse, or you would have been making a trip to the Bissau hospital right now!"

Chapter 15

Heartbreak and Joy as the First Family Come to Faith

Sometimes when treating children there is heartbreak as well as joy. Nmpili was a little girl about six years old who came regularly to Sunday school with her friends. They were playing one day under a huge kapok tree when some bigger boys noticed a wild bees' nest hidden high in the branches.

"We should chase all those bees away," someone suggested. So they started throwing stones at the nest. Of course, they should have sought advice from adults who would have known what to do, but they thought they could do it themselves. Suddenly, all the bees came out with a mighty roar and circled overhead. The children fled for their lives, but Nmpili tripped and fell. The bees descended on her in their thousands. Her screaming and the children shouting in panic brought people running and trying to get past the mass of bees. One elderly man fought his way through, but collapsed on the ground as he got near her. Pastor Domingos came carrying a large blanket. He put it on the ground and crawled underneath it, managing to get Nmpili out. The elderly man was brought to the clinic unconscious. He was only wearing a loin cloth so all the rest of his body was covered with stings. Nmpili, too, was unconscious, dressed only in her knickers, and covered in stings.

We gave antihistamine injections immediately to the man, Nmpili, Domingos, and all the others who had been stung. Then we spent all night trying to remove the stings.

Our two nurses sat beside Nmpili picking out the stings with forceps, while I sat beside the elderly man. To pick out his stings one by one was just impossible, so I scraped them out with my nails for hour after hour. The elderly man recovered consciousness during the night and survived. At six o'clock in the morning Nmpili died.

As I left the distraught family and walked sadly to the house I thought, "What more could we have done?" I picked up a medical book from the book stand, looked up "bee stings", and read, "Do not pick out the stings with forceps. That squeezes the venom in. Scrape them out with a knife."

"Why, oh why," I cried, "why did I not stop and read this first? Why didn't I stop in all the panic and pray? I might have realized that I didn't know what to do." In my ignorance I had done the right thing with the old man, but I had told the nurses to do the wrong thing. I was in charge. It was my responsibility. I was shattered. The boys had acted on their own initiative without consulting others, with terrible consequences. I had done the same thing. We all meant well and had done our best, but there was a better way.

It was too late now. Yes, it was true that Nmpili would almost certainly have died whatever we did as the anaphylactic shock was so great, but that was no comfort.

The lesson was a hard and humbling one to learn, and I needed it.

* * *

One afternoon Dune, our lovely next-door neighbour, came crying to me. "Miss Lily, please come to see Bilopat. He's so ill," she pleaded.

We were very fond of Bilopat, having treated him before for malaria and pneumonia. He was about seven years old and came regularly to Sunday school. He loved to hang around and wash our dishes or do any other little job. I went to their house and there, lying on a straw mat on the verandah, lay the little fellow having a frightening convulsion. I was horrified, recognizing immediately the typical spasm, locked jaw, and high-pitched squeaky voice of tetanus. His head and heels were on the mat, but the rest of his body was in a stiff arch. I sent Dune to fetch Brenda and Domingos. Together we prayed for him, but my faith was almost nil. I had seen too many deaths from this awful infection.

He was trying to say something. Domingos bent over him to listen as he managed to squeak out, "I want to enter Christ." Domingos gently talked with him and it was clear, as he answered "ee, ee" to every question, that he knew what he was doing. He really had understood what had been taught in Sunday school.

As Domingos prayed for him – the prayer he wanted to pray for himself but just couldn't – another cruel spasm ripped through his body. He managed another "ee". We had no anti-tetanus serum, though it would have been useless at this stage. We did what we could, sedating him heavily to stop the spasms and to give him some relief, but little else. Later that evening an aunt arrived, bringing a live chicken to sacrifice to the spirits for his healing. As the family prepared to do this it was obvious that Bilopat didn't agree. They all reasoned with him but Bilopat objected so much and became more distressed. Eventually his father, Pontinta, said, "Leave the child alone. He says he has entered Christ and Christ will heal him." So the aunt went off, complaining loudly, and taking her now very happy live chicken with her.

After a couple of weeks of sedating and tube-feeding him he began to improve. It was truly a miraculous, though slow, healing. Brenda had promised him that she would make him a pair of red shorts when he got better. A few weeks later Dune and Pontinta appeared, walking slowly up our path with Bilopat walking stiffly between them. "I've come for the red shorts you promised," he said.

Bilopat became a strong, vibrant Christian. Three months later Pontinta arrived late one night to see me. "Miss Lily, I've come," he said, followed by a long silence. "I'm going on a canoe journey tomorrow," he continued, pausing again. "I haven't made the sacrifices to the spirits for safety." He eventually explained: "Jesus saved Bilopat so I can trust Jesus now. I want to enter God's way." He knelt and prayed: "Listen to me, man Jesus, I'm finished with it all. You've got to help me. That's it, I'm finished."

When he returned from his journey he was a different man. He had the reputation in the village of being very bad-tempered and violent. Dune, in particular, knew how violent he could be. She was furious when he told her that he had "entered Christ", terrified of the reprisals of the spirits on her and the family. "I'll make him lose his temper," she thought, reasoning that if he became violent and beat her up Christ would reject him. So she decided not to give him the usual meal when he came home from the fields. They ate only once a day so it would be a severe test. But just in case he became too violent with her she hid his dinner under the bed, ready to produce it if he attacked her.

When Pontinta arrived home, tired and hungry, he was told there was no meal. Dune stood defiantly waiting for the outburst. He paused, ready to blow up, and then he remembered that he could ask Jesus to help him. He just ignored her, and went and sat on his bed, struggling to keep calm and pray. Suddenly, he felt his heel clang against something under the bed. He bent and retrieved the dinner. "Thank you, Jesus," he said as he ate it in silence. He returned the empty dish back under the bed, trying not to laugh aloud and shout out his praise to God.

✳ ✳ ✳

The believers all prayed for Dune and two years later, in 1971, she too "entered God's way" at the church's annual conference. There was tremendous rejoicing as the Christian women gathered singing and dancing with her. This was the first family to become Christians. What a wonderful foundation of the church Dune and Pontinta became.

We had started the week-long conferences a few years previously, with the mornings concentrating on learning about the Bible, while in the afternoons there was teaching on practical subjects such as bacteria, first aid, family planning, and agriculture. By 1982 there were 130 adults and eighty children attending the annual conference, sleeping anywhere they could find space in the clinic or in a believer's hut.

One year we had two witchdoctors, Otodo and Noos, baptized in the nearby sea inlet. Noos was about fifty when he was converted and was married in Papel law to two wives. I went to his house and watched him burn a big basket full of witchdoctor equipment and he kept praying, "Jesus Christ, this is in Your name." But there was a cost to him becoming a Christian. His first wife went off with his brother, which is serious incest in Papel law. He had to evict her from their home and he could have her back only if he performed a foul witchcraft ritual and animal sacrifices.

She had pleaded for him to take her back but she was not a Christian. Noos wanted her back but now as a Christian he could not perform this ceremony, nor should he have two wives if he could honourably dismiss one. However, to dismiss her would force her into prostitution as no man would dare to marry her. Another problem was that witchdoctors become very rich through their work.

When they become Christians all their income stops and they have to find other work, which can be very difficult. I thought I'd never had counselling difficulties like this back home in Liverpool, and I prayed the elders of the church would have real wisdom from God as they sorted this problem out.

At the conference each new Christian gave a testimony to the gathered crowd. The baptism candidates, including the witchdoctors, were so enthusiastically long-winded that by the time they had all finished the tide had gone out. Pastor Domingos, the baptism candidates, and all the church members then had a long trip to the sea to find enough water for the baptism.

Chapter 16

It Shouldn't Happen to a Veteran Missionary

Brenda had a vision. She was keen to produce some of our own food and improve our diet. Every rainy season Brenda planted peanuts, but the boys who harvested them for us ate plenty, and the girls who shelled and roasted them had their share too. In the end, we had hardly any more nuts than we had planted. Vegetables fared badly too as the neighbours' goats and cows ate the small plants as soon as they appeared. The cows were adept at putting their horns through the wire netting fence and pulling it up. Also, the nails securing the netting attracted thieves and never stayed there very long.

Fruit trees, too, were a problem. We had a fruitful lemon tree near the well where the women came to draw water. Some imagined that the fruit was a gift to them, so we often had to buy our own lemons in the market. We had two orange trees, but we never ate an orange off them as they all disappeared before they were ripe. Our efforts to stop people taking our mango fruit led to arguments and a lot of unpleasantness. One lady even helped herself to a sack full of mangoes one night and took them to sell in Bissau. Again and again the Lord had to remind us that we really have no rights. And anyway, their needs were greater than ours.

✳ ✳ ✳

As for the animals, our obstetric knowledge didn't really suffice. First, there were the chickens. They always seemed to get some sickness and die just when they began to lay eggs. Then Brenda decided to try ducks. On one occasion we had a hen sitting on eggs, and a duck sitting on her eggs at the same time. The mother duck died before her eggs hatched. Brenda reasoned that ducklings were more valuable than chicks so she put the duck eggs under the hen and transferred the hen's eggs to a box with straw and a paraffin lamp underneath. It bore some slight resemblance to an incubator. In case the hen with her duck eggs or the "incubator" were stolen we put them in the locked outside toilet. Brenda stuck a note on the door saying, "Please remember to turn these eggs over every time you come in here." We had noticed that hens turned their eggs frequently during the incubation. Both the chicks and ducklings hatched out, and surprisingly, the mother hen adopted both the chicks and the ducklings.

It might have been a great idea had it not been the rainy season, when deep streams ran through our compound. The ducklings were delighted and frolicked excitedly in the water as it flowed down toward the road. Meanwhile, the mother hen was distraught – cluck, cluck, clucking, with wings flapping, desperately trying, in vain, to get her abnormal "chicks" to come out of the water.

The other hens looked on in amazement and helped with the clucking. Then Brenda or I had to rush to the rescue, getting drenched in the process.

We eventually reared twenty-three ducks who followed Brenda everywhere, leaving their "visiting cards" when I tried to chase them out of the house. However, twenty-two ducks died from sickness, leaving just one who survived. We called her Elijah, after the Old Testament prophet who had said, "I am the only one of the Lord's prophets left" (1 Kings 18:22). We reckoned that a lady duck wouldn't have minded having a male name.

Then Brenda tried to rear rabbits. We bought a pair from Senegal and we made them a pleasant hutch. After a lot of care, and doing all the right things according to the instruction manual, we discovered that they were both males! So, undaunted, Brenda bought a female. We were both excited when the female rabbit produced four bunnies. Sadly, one slipped through the netting and was eaten by our dog, and another died. Then when the other two had grown Brenda steeled herself to kill one. After all, the whole idea was to enhance our diet. However, none of us enjoyed eating it. I finally gave the fourth one away when Brenda went on leave, but she didn't thank me!

✳ ✳ ✳

One day Brenda made a coop and fenced it off to keep her treasured family of a dozen or more hens safe from theft and isolated from the diseases that the nearby hens had. When she went on leave I was entrusted with them.

"We are having visitors," I said to Quinta, my helper, one day. "Please kill a chicken and cook it for me."

"You haven't got any chickens," she said.

"There are a dozen or more in the pen," I replied, "I've been feeding them every day."

"No, those all belong to neighbours who asked me to put them in the pen to keep them safe," she explained.

"Then where are Miss Brenda's?" I asked.

"Oh, some died and some were stolen; there are none left," she replied, as though it was the most natural thing in the world, and what was I worrying about. I wondered how she was so sure it was our hens that had died and not the neighbours' hens.

* * *

One of our Christian neighbours had a pig that became sick and died. She agreed to let us bury the dead pig, which we did. Two nights later we heard a commotion in the garden and found a group of women busy digging up the dead pig to eat it.

"No, no," I tried to explain, "if you eat that meat you could die of the sickness that killed the pig."

They were annoyed and grumbled among themselves. "No, I'm not being mean or hard-hearted," I protested, but I couldn't convince them. They had always eaten the meat of an animal that died.

"We haven't got sick or died," they reasoned. "We could sell it in the market and make money." I stood my ground, explaining all the dangers and refusing to give in to them. They went off unconvinced. Maybe that was why sometimes I had the nickname "*Tambkeni*", tight-fisted.

Later, we discovered that nobody ever killed a cow or a goat just to sell or eat it. They were all reared only for sacrificing in the rituals and at funerals. Any meat offered for sale in the market, or at our door, was from an animal that had died from a sickness.

However, on one occasion we were offered wild meat that was from an animal that had been killed by a leopard or hyena. We cooked it in anticipation of a lovely meat meal. It tasted horrible, probably due to the hormones that were released as it died. We never bought any meat in Biombo ever again.

✳✳✳

Brenda bought a piglet, a sweet, clean, intelligent pet called Miss Piggy. She, too, followed Brenda everywhere. As she grew bigger and hungrier it was a struggle to find food for her. Eventually, we agreed to have her killed which, of course, was Brenda's original intention. Miss Piggy became a good meal and some strings of sausages. But we didn't enjoy either the sausages or the meat, though our African helpers did.

Then Brenda couldn't resist taking in a neighbour's pathetic puppy. It was covered with sores and full of fleas but responded to her tender care. Sadly it got rabies, but before it bit anyone I had the miserable job of giving it the fatal injection of animal euthanasia.

✳✳✳

Animal husbandry was certainly not our calling. But how could I refuse to go to see our neighbour's precious cow, which, he said, was all swollen following the birth of a calf. All he had was invested in that cow. When I saw the poor animal it reminded me of a similar case in the famous TV series *It Shouldn't Happen to a Vet*. In that programme James Herriot had treated a cow with calcium.

So I gave the cow a large injection of calcium. It improved, so the next day I gave it another – the last one I had. The cow improved some more, but a week later it deteriorated. I had no more calcium and the cow died. I went to say how sorry I was to the neighbour. "Don't worry," he said kindly. "It had to die. It is God's will."

That isn't quite my theology, I thought, as I silently argued with God.

✳ ✳ ✳

Another time a group of men came with a cow that had been viciously attacked for eating the young rice in a neighbour's paddy field. She had a long, deep gash in her side. "I can't help you," I said. "I'm not a vet." But they wouldn't give up pleading, "Please stitch it up or she will die." I was sorry for the man and his precious cow so I gave in.

We went for the largest suture needle we could find and the strongest thread. We insisted that the cow was tied securely to a tree and held by the men. She mooed and moaned as we stitched the soft red flesh with dissoluble thread, but when we tried to push the needle through the tough hide she really howled, struggled, and fought for her life. The men tried to sit on her but she threw them off and rolled in the dirt, bellowing furiously. Eventually, spattered with mud and blood, and collecting a large audience, we put twenty stitches in her hide. Any semblance of sterility had been abandoned, so we gave her God's needle and a huge, long-lasting injection of penicillin. She recovered and healed well, but they never brought her back to have the stitches out, for which I was thankful.

There were other similar "patients", such as a cow with obstructed labour for three days. What could we do? I didn't know the anatomy of a cow, but tried anyway, locating the legs of the calf and pulling with all my might – all to no avail. The cow died. Brenda, however, was more successful when she responded to a call to go to a cow in obstructed labour. She was able to detect some suitable part of its anatomy and managed to deliver it with the vacuum extractor. Miraculously, both calf and mother survived.

✳ ✳ ✳

Later Brenda's mum came to visit us. What a joy that was for us and I'm sure she thoroughly enjoyed it too. She made lovely meals and happily took care of the livestock, especially the hens, who made friends with her, wandering in and out of her bedroom. Brenda objected, but her mum thought they were so cute. Several times her mum mentioned she had itching at night, but it was only after she had left us that we found a batch of tiny, almost microscopic hen fleas in her bed. We hoped she didn't take any home with her.

Her sister Mary also visited us during the rainy season. She was a great gardener so she enjoyed planting and tending some tomato seeds and other vegetables. They thrived well under her tender care, but one morning Mary came to Brenda, crying, "The neighbours' goats have got in and they've eaten the lot!"

After all this work with animals someone suggested that Brenda or I should find a vet in England, marry him, and bring him back to be the first ever vet in the country. Good idea, we thought. But perhaps we didn't try hard enough!

Chapter 17

Bridging a Gap as Dentists

We didn't just try our hand at all creatures great and small; we also experimented with dentistry. When I was home on my first leave I visited my dentist, Mr Turner, in Walton, Liverpool. He reluctantly relieved me of all my teeth, saying it was more than necessary and was amazed that I had never had toothache. That was a miracle in itself. As compensation for my loss he gave me a lovely set of dental forceps to take back to Africa. Brenda and I were thrilled – but who would have the courage to use them? Very often patients came to us in agony with their rotten teeth. Some older people had suffered for years until none or only one tooth remained, the rest having dropped out. All we could do was to give aspirin tablets. But now we had this challenge.

"Go on, Lily, you do it," Brenda said to me one day when a boy of about sixteen pleaded with us to pull out his aching tooth. We arranged a "dental chair", which was a wooden box placed horizontally. Pedrinho stood behind holding the boy's head. I gripped the gums with one hand, put the forceps firmly on the offending tooth, and wriggled it slightly, whereupon the boy screamed, grasped both my wrists, and wrapped his legs around my waist. I hung on fast until he finally escaped and I was left holding the tooth in the forceps. He was off down the path at full speed and I never saw him again. Perhaps we would have done better finding a dentist in England to join the vet we needed, and had a double wedding!

* * *

After a few similar harrowing experiences we sent off to England for instructions on giving a local anaesthetic. This proved to be a great help. Brenda became our senior dentist and had some desperate and grateful patients almost every day. She taught our senior nurse, Tiago, and he became the only dentist, or rather "Extractor of Teeth", for miles around and, at times, the only one in the whole country.

However, there was one very distressing experience when we extracted a tooth from Sanha, who was a witchdoctor, an important leader in his tribe, and a blacksmith in a village 3 miles away. He developed what seemed to be a dry socket, which, in spite of treatment, became worse and worse. All our efforts and prayers were in vain, as were all the incantations and animal sacrifices he made to the spirits.

After several weeks the ulceration appeared to be cancerous and had spread around his face, leaving a gaping hole. He was very ill. We went every day to dress his face and tube-feed him. It was such an ordeal, but in it all the Lord Jesus met with him. Sanha gave up the spirit worship and began to listen eagerly as we shared the gospel with him each day.

"Today I'm going to enter Christ's way," he said to us one day. So Pastor Domingos led him to the Lord. It was real! It was evident! He tried to smile and sing as best he could. He was a changed man, eager to tell his family, and was obviously at peace.

When Brenda went to him a few days later, just before Easter, he sang a song he had made up. It went: "I am Sanha. I was lost. Now I am in Christ's way. Jesus died and rose from the dead at Easter time. Sanha will die and rise from the dead this Easter time too. I will go to heaven and live with him."

He died on Easter Day morning. As he was a very important man the funeral had to be held according to all the tribal customs, and people came from far and wide with numerous animals slaughtered in sacrifice. The body was wrapped ceremoniously in many layers of cloths, becoming enormous. The wailing, drumming, and spirit-possessed dancing went on for days. The fire-water flowed freely until even the young drummer boys were rolling drunk. When it was time for the burial they conceded that it would be permissible for Pastor Domingos to perform the Christian ceremony as well. So Domingos took the opportunity of preaching the gospel to the many people who stood around.

The body was placed in a bier made of wood branches and carried on the shoulders of four men. It was to be questioned by a head witchdoctor. Domingos urged them to just take it to the grave, explaining that there could be no answer as Sanha was no longer there but was in heaven. They ignored him. Domingos stood his ground and declared loudly, "There will be no answer."

It was an intense, awesome spiritual battle. The powers of darkness were almost tangible, and I thought of Elijah in the Old Testament and his battle with the 450 prophets of Baal on Mount Carmel. They asked question after question, but instead of the bier lurching around the circle, as they expected, it stayed perfectly motionless. None of the spirit mediums present could fake an answer to a question, though they were certainly experienced in doing this.

Eventually, they gave in and the exhausted bearers proceeded to carry the bier across a small field to the grave. As it neared the open grave it suddenly turned round and seemed to be dragging the bearers at a speed, back to the house. Then, instead of going through the normal opening in the hedge, it pulled the bearers through the thick, thorny bushes, cutting their legs and arms. The crowd went wild with delight. "Sanha has come back to be questioned," they shouted triumphantly.

With his hands raised to heaven Domingos cried out in a loud shout, "In the Name of Jesus there will be no answer."

They tried to repeat the performance, but each question met with a breathless silence. God had shut their mouths. It was awesome! The exhausted bearers were eventually given permission to carry the bier to the grave and bury Sanha's body. Quietly, the crowd gradually dispersed and slowly made their way home. Today there are many believers and an active growing church in that village.

Chapter 18

Tensions over whether to Treat or to Translate

During Christmas 1973 I was looking forward to going home on furlough in the next couple of months. At the time I looked back at my work since returning to Biombo after my previous visit to Liverpool. "Your job is to learn the Papel language, turn it into a written language, and translate the New Testament," Leslie Brierley, our field leader, had instructed me when I first set out for the Papel tribe.

If it seemed impossible then, it was even more impossible now. I had made a tentative alphabet and translated some Bible stories. But as I delved deeper it became so complicated and the alphabet needed revising. The grammatical structure of the language was fascinating, but there was nobody to explain it to me, and it needed hours of work and research to get it right. Word divisions alone were such a headache. Where should I put all the spaces? What were words in themselves and what were suffixes or prefixes? I found that Papel has ten different classes, or genders. For example, instead of having just he, she, and it the pronoun changes in accordance with the class of the noun and likewise the adjective and whole sentence. Of course, the people had no difficulty with it, but I certainly did. Yes, I knew with God that nothing is impossible, but perhaps Leslie had got it wrong and I'm not up to the task intellectually.

"I just can't do it," I said to Brenda one day. "I think the Lord is telling me to give up the language work and not worry about it any more. To translate the New Testament into Papel is completely beyond me." She didn't agree. Yet I knew I couldn't continue to do both translation and medicine. Nor could I leave all the medical work to Brenda. We prayed about it, of course. Shortly afterwards we had a delivery of mail and in it a card from England. It was bright red with large black writing that just said, "I can do all things through Christ who strengthens me" (Philippians 4:13, NKJV).

The card said nothing else but it was enough. Jesus had spoken to me. Somehow He would enable me, and in the meantime I did what I could and didn't worry about the rest.

The church work was also taking up more and more time as new people arrived, so there were now around forty meeting every Sunday. The recent converts were so eager to learn and they were a joy to teach. Domingos, Armando, and Pedrinho, who had really matured, just lapped up anything we could teach them. With great enthusiasm they took over most of the evangelistic outreach and organizing the church affairs and services. Domingos was a natural pastor. He was an amazing man, full of the Holy Spirit and had wisdom far beyond his years.

The predictions of some of my colleagues in Bissau were also proving true. The medical work had grown. More and more desperate, needy people came for help until we were treating more than 200 patients each day, with people noisily queuing for the clinic on the verandah near my bedroom from 3 a.m. The primitive maternity unit was becoming famous, which meant day and night work. Yes, the medical work had become the priority over the translation work.

When Brenda needed to spend time in Bissau making and duplicating the reading primers she had prepared, our field leader sent Thelma Mills to help me. I was delighted, as I was physically tired and spiritually low. I felt I couldn't face being alone. Of course, it wouldn't mean being really alone as we were helped by our hard-working and trusted team. But spiritually I was dry and more needy than I realized. It was the rainy season which meant there were many more patients in the clinic, more night call-outs and multitudes of mosquitoes. It also seemed to be that every night there were complications in the maternity unit. My own prayer time was non-existent and the church prayer meetings were, to me, a dutiful burden. I would much rather have gone to bed.

Knowing how enthusiastic Thelma was, my expectations ran high. "Thelma loves to get the chance to practise some midwifery," I selfishly thought, "so she can have all the night deliveries and I can get some sleep." When she arrived she shared with me how the Lord had spoken to her about her lack of prayer. "I've been challenged," she said, "by Ecclesiastes 8:3: 'Do not be in a hurry to leave the king's presence.'"

My heart sank when she suggested we spend unhurried time together in prayer. That was not what I wanted, and my face must have betrayed me, so she waited until the next day. The usual Tuesday night weekly church prayer meeting finished about 10 o'clock when she asked, "Can we pray now?" I answered abruptly, "I don't pray on a Tuesday night." Her face fell. So I said, "All right then, but make it short."

On Wednesday night I had no excuse. We prayed. Or, more correctly, Thelma prayed. I tried to keep it short. Deep down I knew my trouble wasn't just physical tiredness. For months I had drifted, working hard and dutifully in my own strength and was spiritually burnt out. I couldn't go on like this. The next night we looked into the book of Esther and were challenged by the question, "What is it, Queen Esther? What is your request? Even up to half the kingdom, it will be given you" (5:3).

What did I really want? In desperation my heart cried out, "It is you, Jesus, your love alone. That is all I want." Our experience during those following nights was impossible to put into words. We read the Song of Songs together, seeing it in a new, personal, and intimate way. God's love burned in my heart. It was real and overwhelming. Time didn't seem to matter any more. We certainly weren't in a hurry to leave His presence. This was the banqueting house and we were under His banner of love. "I am my beloved's and my beloved is mine" (Song of Solomon 6:3). This was a reality then; it still is and will be for ever. Praise and worship were paramount, even during the duties of each day.

An amazing thing happened. We didn't have a single night maternity case nor a village call-out for the whole two weeks. Afterwards, we heard that there had been four women who had delivered their babies on the way to our maternity unit and had turned round and taken their little bundles of joy home.

The prayer sessions with Thelma were just what I needed to rejuvenate my spirit and remind me of why I was in this faraway country. I marvelled at Jesus' graciousness in loving me despite my weaknesses and felt inspired to write about it:

> However can such wonder be
> That Jesus is in love with me?
> Where is that beauty seen by Him
> In one so weak and stained with sin?
> Can he a faint reflection see
> As in a glass He looks at me?

***

After Thelma had returned to Bissau we had the joy of welcoming Marjorie Gowland, from Gateshead, when she came to Guinea-Bissau as a full-time WEC missionary. The country had refused all visa applications for seven years, so it was a miracle that she was given hers. Brenda was due to go on furlough soon so Marjorie was much needed. The big question was: would she be able to join us, or would she be assigned to another area in the country? When she realized what was involved, would she want to come? We were delighted when, after a short time of orientation in the capital, Marjorie did indeed join us in early 1972.

She turned out to be all we could have hoped for. She soon adapted to our primitive, old-fashioned methods, though with some painful adjustments. Her midwifery and general nursing training were much more up to date, but the equipment that is so available in an English hospital was sadly lacking. Marjorie took it all in her stride. The long hours, disturbed nights, and frequent emergencies didn't seem to faze her. She loved Jesus and inspired us.

After Brenda returned we started having a day off each week as far as possible, and a rota for the night calls. It made such a difference and I could now have more time to concentrate on translation. But Brenda and I sometimes forgot we were a team of three. A while later Marjorie graciously shared with us that she felt left out and not needed. It was a wake-up call. Brenda and I had become so used to sharing decisions, problems, and fellowship together that we hadn't included her. We needed this rebuke. It was from the Lord. "A cord of three strands is not quickly broken", says Ecclesiastes 4:12. This proved true. All three strands have to be equal, each one is needed, and they must be bound together.

Several lovely things stand out in my memory of our time with Marjorie. One morning when we were working together, I was consulting patients in a very busy clinic. We had been there for five hours and I was getting more and more uptight and irritated, especially with the men who couldn't see why they should sit in the queue waiting their turn. In their culture men never sat and waited with the women and children. They thought they had every right to walk straight to the front of the queue and be treated immediately. In my culture it isn't so! We clashed.

Marjorie was treating the patients who had stinking leg ulcer wounds. They were sitting on the verandah outside my open window so she could hear all that was going on. My voice was raised and I was angry. She walked in, and without a word, put a piece of paper on my desk and walked out. When I looked at it I read just three words: "For you, Jesus". I've never forgotten that piece of paper. To my shame there have been many other times when I have needed it.

✳ ✳ ✳

Another time Marjorie and I had to travel to Bissau for our missionary conference. We had had a busy night and were tired and weary. We set out early to catch the daily rickety bus for the eight-hour journey. A man met us with the customary greeting: "I greet you. How is your body? Where are you going?" No one ever talks about the weather in Guinea-Bissau.

"To Bissau," I explained.

"Don't go on the bus," he said. "It is very sick; it will die on the way." It certainly looked sick, but we decided we had to risk it.

After a few miles the driver had to stop to find some water to pour over the wheels and engine. The bus was unbearably hot, so we got out and sat on the verandah of a nearby house. I felt strangely stirred and excited.

Somehow, in some lovely, unusual way I felt the presence of Jesus. Marjorie, never at a loss for words, was unusually silent. "It's strange," I said, "somehow I feel… different."

"Yes," Marjorie replied as she fumbled for words. "I know what you mean. It's Jesus, isn't it? He is with us."

* * *

When the driver called we returned to the bus. It bumped, rattled, and snorted for another few miles. The floor was so hot I was afraid my plastic sandals would melt, so I tried to keep my feet up. I felt sorry for a woman's chicken on the floor with its legs tied together, but I was somewhat elated and, strangely for me, not at all sorry for myself. A deep sense of joy was overwhelming me. I wanted to get up and dance. So it was no hardship when the bus finally died and we all had to get out, find a village, and wait for tomorrow's bus.

We were about 15 miles away from the city. The red sandy road stretched out before us as far as the eye could see. There was not a scrap of shade. The midday sun shone in all its cruel, relentless splendour, and we had carelessly forgotten to bring water or a sunshade.

"Let's walk; we can make 15 miles before dark," we decided. So we set off and found ourselves walking, or rather dancing, singing, and praising Jesus, as though we were on the way to heaven. We talked to each other and to Jesus, and He talked with us, in a three-way conversation, punctuated with songs and tongues of worship. "Oh my God," I cried in all reverence, "I've never experienced anything like this before." Nor has either of us since. His presence was almost tangible. We were overwhelmed, totally drunk with a cocktail of love, joy, and peace. The miles passed unnoticed. We could have continued walking right into heaven.

After about 12 miles we arrived at a small village that had a tavern and realized, for the first time, that we were hot, wet with sweat, and thirsty. The kindly tavern owner brought us each a tin of Fanta, which was like the nectar of heaven. I took off my sandals and found that I had several blisters on my feet and hadn't felt them. A couple of miles further on a car stopped to give us a lift to our headquarters. We thanked Jesus, but we were glad the car hadn't come any earlier!

I don't know why we were given this precious, undeserved, and even unsought for experience. Perhaps it was our Emmaus road experience, similar to when Jesus met with two of his disciples after His resurrection. Hopefully, it will be like this when I reach that final shining highway to heaven.

Chapter 19

Sadness as Dad Dies

For me 1974 had started so well, as we the missionaries and church members enjoyed a New Year's Day picnic on the man-made beach at the sea 4 miles away. But our celebrations were interrupted by our mission leader Gene McBride arriving from Bissau to tell me the sad news that my Dad had died earlier that morning. I immediately packed my bags and made plans to fly home to the UK, although I thought I would arrive too late for the funeral.

At Christmas my parents had sent me, as usual, a tape with family news on it. I was intrigued by my dad's comment: "Lily, I've gone religious." My mum quickly changed the subject and wouldn't let him say any more. When I met a friend who had been at the funeral she told me of a conversation she had had with Dad. A fortnight before he died he had bought a new car, to which my friend said, "You can't take that with you when you go."

He replied, "I know I can't, but I have got what I can take with me."

I believe Dad did come to faith in those last few months of his life and it made it slightly easier for me coming home.

***

I stayed with Mum about nine months, and during that time I was able to buy a car to take back with me to Biombo. What joy: it had been our dream for more than fifteen years! "Oh, to have our own car…" was my cry when we had a mother urgently needing a Caesarean operation or who was bleeding badly. In comparison, the journey to the Bissau hospital on the old bus or an open truck was horrific.

So I was thrilled to bring back a new VW Combi. I had booked it on the car ferry, The Eagle, travelling from Southampton to Lisbon. There were some setbacks and it seemed that the paperwork would not be through in time for the sailing. My Liverpool church really prayed and I took a stand of faith that our precious car would sail. Then one of the men, Tom, said, "I feel that the Lord is saying that the car is not going to be on the boat." I felt he must be wrong. I went to Southampton docks fully expecting to see the car ready to be loaded on board. It wasn't. We sailed without it.

In the Bay of Biscay we hit a storm. It was a hurricane force 12 which raged for two full days. The noise was horrendous as huge vehicles on the car deck broke loose and crashed into one another. A tanker of spirit broke up; its flammable load flowed all over the deck. A furniture van full of antique furniture was reduced to rubble, a lorry of frozen food scattered its contents of peas, cauliflower, and chips over the deck, and a lovely new caravan was concertinaed. It was horrific. About ten vehicles were destroyed and many other badly damaged.

There could be no cooking, so the stewards brought us sandwiches and milk, but I couldn't face them. Sleep was impossible. Nor could I get off my bunk. As the ship rolled I found myself upright with my back against the bunk and my feet on the wall. Then, as the ship rolled back again, I was standing on my head.

When we finally reached Lisbon, two days late, we saw the damage to the ship. It was terrible. I just gasped as I saw the damaged vehicles lined up at the docks together with the heaps of rubble that had once been people's luggage. I was so relieved my luggage had only slight damage. How I thanked God for his protection – no lives were lost, though there were some injuries.

Thankfully, our car was not on the ship! That too would have been rubble. It arrived safely a few weeks later. As I drove back to Biombo I sang a new song:

> My times are in Your hands,
> My God I leave them there.
> Why should I clutter up my life
> With faithless anxious care?
> The future is not changed
> However hard I fret.
> Why spoil the joy of now
> With what's not happened yet?

A new garage was built with a tin roof and a window. Didi, one of our church elders, gazed at it and said wistfully, "What a magnificent house for a car." He was doubtless thinking of his own windowless mud hut with a straw roof.

However, when Areta, the lovely wife of our field leader, Gene McBride, was badly injured when the only other mission vehicle in Bissau was written off in a crash, our new VW was sent to the capital where it was desperately needed to ferry goods and personnel around. It was with a heavy heart that we waved it off – and it would be another twelve months before it returned.

Chapter 20

The Night a Naked Man Arrived with an Idol

"Lily, wake up!" Brenda yelled at me. "It's 2 a.m. and the lights on the car keep going on and off." After a year in Bissau the VW had now at last arrived back in Biombo long-term. It was parked outside Brenda's bedroom window and, yes, I agreed the lights were strangely flashing on and off. So we went out to investigate. To our amazement a young man was sitting in the driver's seat trying to start the engine. I opened the door and ordered him out. He was stark naked.

"Whatever are you doing?" I asked.

"I'm taking the god to Quetaha," he replied.

"You had better go home first and get some clothes on," I said, helping him out. Surprisingly, he obeyed and off he went. We opened the rear door and sure enough there was the idol of the fearful Papel god. We wondered how he had managed to carry it the considerable distance from the temple to our compound.

Every village had one or two of these temples with a god in each. There was nothing to indicate that it was indeed a temple, as it was just a straw roof on poles, measuring about 3 metres by 2 metres and with a hard mud floor. The straw roof hung so low it was necessary to bend down to see inside, where there were a few clay pots in which offerings of food or fire-water had been left. Several bits of blood-stained cloth lay around. Hanging by ropes from the roof was an oblong object measuring about a metre long wrapped in a red, blood-stained blanket. It had long carrying poles running through it and a small bell hung from it. This was their god.

In Papel culture each god is considered extremely powerful and fearful. Strange too that about every seventh year this god grows weak and loses power. It then has to be taken to the nearby island of Pecixe to be re-empowered. We never found out why the naked man was taking the god to the village of Quetaha, but it was probably to cure a sick person there.

This god has some faint resemblance to the ark of the covenant of the Old Testament. It is consulted over serious sicknesses, guidance and safety on journeys, curses, and crops and appeased with animal sacrifices. Only certain men can approach it and carry it. "Whatever should we do with it?" we thought. We don't want it here until morning. So we hauled it out of our vehicle and carried it between us down the road. Brenda started singing:

> There is power, power, wonder working power
> in the precious blood of the Lamb...

Together we sang as we walked to the village centre and deposited the god in the middle of the dirt road. It was a strategic place where people gathered for the market, the tavern shops, and the bus terminus. It was a dark, moonless night so nobody saw or heard us. We made our way back to bed like a couple of giggling schoolgirls, wondering what would happen when the people found it in the morning.

Next day there was uproar. Nobody could pass the god for fear of their lives. "Who did this?" they asked. Eventually, when the truth came out, people could hardly believe it and there were many predictions of what terrible fate awaited us. Of course, nothing happened to us and the delighted Christians pointed out the great power of Jesus compared to the impotence of their so-called god.

However, dealing with their fears and beliefs in the spirits that supposedly inhabited the idols was a fairly regular occurrence for us. I was once asked to go to a home where a young woman was very ill. It was difficult to get information about her and Pastor Domingos was suspicious that there was more to it than the relatives were telling us, so he came with me. Sure enough, it seemed very serious when we saw crowds of people standing silently around. Domingos told me, "You wait here while I go in the house."

As he stood on the threshold I heard him declare loudly, "Take this idol out now. We will not come in until you do." There followed a lot of arguing and shouting, but Domingos stood his ground and then prayed in a loud voice for Jesus to show His power over this so-called god and all the powers of Satan.

Eventually and reluctantly they brought the god from out of the room where it had been beside the young woman. The people scattered in fear as it was put outside the house.

Domingos called me to go in with him. I was anxious, wondering whether the young woman would be already dead, or whether I would be able to cope. I saw that she was obviously very ill and had been deteriorating over a long time. She was unable to answer my questions and I couldn't trust what the family said.

I felt death was imminent; I suspected she was in the final stage of tuberculosis which was so prevalent in the Biombo area. Indeed, in almost every extended family dwelling there was at least one person suffering or dying with untreated tuberculosis. It was hopeless, but I did what I could to satisfy the relatives, and gave her an anti-malarial injection and antibiotics with God's needle.

Domingos prayed for her healing and we left, leaving the rest with the Lord.

The next day we found that the idol had been taken back to its temple and the young woman was much improved. Miraculously, with a few more days of treatment and nourishing milk drinks, she completely recovered. God had honoured Domingos' prayer of faith and some more seeds were sown in people's hearts.

***

Another story concerned an old man named Media, who had been trying to clean an empty petrol drum to store water when he dropped some burning straw into it. The whole drum exploded and left him blind, scarred, and asthmatic. He came to us frequently for treatment, holding on to the end of a long stick, led by his young son. As Media heard the gospel many times he began asking questions. "Would Jesus give me my sight back?" Would He? I was glad that Domingos answered that question and not me. Media was totally dependent on his three wives for everything, so to enter Christ and be rejected by the whole extended family was quite out of the question. However, he kept coming to the clinic and lapping up the teaching.

Very early one morning we heard Media gasping desperately outside our window. "I've come to enter Christ," he cried. He was really in a bad way with a severe asthmatic attack and he thought he was dying. After praying with him we treated his asthma and he went home rejoicing – and breathing more easily.

That afternoon we went to his house with Domingos and a few believers, expecting to see him burn all his many spirit fetishes and charms connected with the local gods. Instead, we saw an angry family group with Media sitting in the middle of them in tears. "I can't do it," he said. "My wives are all going to leave me. My grown-up sons and all the family are ready to kill me if I don't leave Christ's way. I can't stay in Christ's way any more. I've come out."

Silently and sadly we made our way home. As the weeks passed Media kept coming for treatment for his asthma, but he was so miserable. While Domingos was preaching to the other patients in the clinic he sat a distance away, always out of hearing.

However, some weeks later, we again had a desperate, dying Media battering at our door in the early hours, shouting between the gasps that he wanted to enter Christ's way now. After we prayed with him and treated him again he calmed down. "Now if they kill me I will go to heaven and be with Jesus," he said.

When we went to his home that afternoon we met a triumphant Media with all his fetishes in a heap ready to be burnt. He lit a fire and threw them all on, including the sacred sticks and bits of cloth. As he smashed each clay pot he cried, "In the name of Jesus." The family were silent, obviously upset, but there were very few repercussions. Later, one by one, his three wives were all converted and all his children. Media is in heaven now, with perfect sight.

***

Armando Pereira was a young man living in Dorse, a small village about 3 miles away. He was an alcoholic and broke the hearts of his wife, Maria Augusta, and his mother. He stole from them and anyone else to provide for the fire-water, the local potent drink to which he was addicted. One day he reached rock bottom and went out with a rope, tied it high in a tree, and was about to tie the other end round his neck and jump.

Suddenly, a man passing through the woods saw him and persuaded him to come down. "The Christ people can set you free," he said. So Armando was persuaded to come to us for help. Pastor Domingos prayed with him and he was converted and he stopped drinking. Armando thrived, attending every meeting, even though it meant a 3-mile walk each way. He was the first convert in his village and testified to his family, neighbours, and friends.

Then tragedy! At a funeral he was persuaded to drink the fire-water again, and slipped right back, becoming even more violent than before with his wife. His mother, in desperation, came to Domingos. "Please, please," she begged, falling on the ground before him, "come and get him back in Christ. He was so lovely when he was in Christ's way and now he is a wild villain." Domingos went home with her, found a truly repentant Armando, and was able to assure him of forgiveness and restoration. He never drank the fire-water again. His mother and wife were also later converted, and a church was planted in his village with Armando himself as their very able pastor. But that wasn't the end of all their problems.

Armando and Maria Augusta had two daughters, Sabado and Camboda. Sabado married a Christian but Camboda refused a suitor who said he was a Christian. Her father asked her why she was refusing him. "Dad," she said, "I am a virgin. I love Jesus, so how can I give him what he is demanding from me now before we get married? He is not the man for me!" Camboda had many bad teeth that needed to be extracted. She heard that there was a dentist in a small town a couple of days' journey away who was able, at a price, to fit false teeth. So she worked and saved until she had enough money to make the journey.

She was away a week when Pastor Domingos heard on the local radio that a girl called Camboda had died, and the body was being returned to her family in Biombo.

We rushed to their village. They had heard the news as well and, like us, were sure there was a mistake. We waited all day until eventually a truck arrived carrying a body in the back. It was Camboda, fully dressed and wearing a pretty, but blood-stained, dress. Her mouth and face were bloodied, but the new, complete set of teeth was in place. The men who brought her knew nothing of how or why she had died. There was no paperwork and no means of finding out. How my heart cried out for the parents.

All the villagers who had gathered began the traditional wailing and crying. We sat with them each day and throughout the funeral. It was grim. The extended family and the tribal elders insisted on holding a Papel funeral with the witchcraft ceremonies and animal sacrifices. All the protests of Armando were in vain. He refused to take part, as the father of the deceased should have done. This led to fierce arguments and bitterness. "Camboda is in heaven with Jesus," Armando declared. "You can't do anything to her now." They did, in the end, allow Domingos to preach to the vast crowd. Miraculously, the noise stopped as he began and they all listened in silence.

The following Sunday Armando unexpectedly walked to the front of the Biombo church with his head held high, and with a clear voice he declared, "God has blessed me with two lovely daughters. Both love Jesus. One was married as a virgin; my other daughter has joined the 144,000 virgins that surround the throne of Jesus. I want to thank Him before you all." His theology may have been unorthodox, but his heart was right. There were many tears shed that morning.

Chapter 21

Lost in Translation

Having Marjorie's extra help in the clinic meant I could work part-time on the Bible translation. I did the majority with Domingos, but it was very slow as I had to work primarily from the Portuguese translation of the New Testament. As he knew only a little Portuguese I needed to explain it in Creole. When I was sure he really understood it he would then translate it into Papel.

I would work on a chapter and then type it out. The next day we would check it and alter or improve parts. I would type it out again. The following day we would check that, make more alterations, and then I would type the whole page again. Sometimes I would say, "But that is what we had originally."

"Yes," he would say, "but the original was better." So I would type the page again. Then I'd make carbon copies of a whole Gospel or epistle for others to read to see if they understood it. Where the meaning wasn't clear it meant discussing it and typing it out again. With the barriers of four languages it was not surprising that some things were lost in translation.

* * *

When Pedrinho was reading from the first duplicated draft of Luke, chapter 22, he said, "Miss Lily, I can't understand this: why did the disciples throw stones at Jesus?"

"No, they didn't," I replied.

"Yes they did," he said, "and he was praying too."

I looked over his shoulder as he traced his stump of a finger along the lines. "Look," he read triumphantly, "Jesus went to pray at a place where the disciples could throw stones at him." We had translated the phrase as it is in the Portuguese King James Version literally: "He went a stone's throw away from them." Thanks to Pedrinho it now reads, "The place where Jesus prayed was not far from where the disciples sat." Even after we had done all the typing, checking, and retyping nobody else had picked that up.

So often, language similarities can be misinterpreted. In Mark 5:41, Domingos had interpreted *Talita cumi* (Little girl, get up) as *Talita, kumi* (Talita, eat!) because the word *kumi* in Portuguese Creole meant "eat", so Domingos reasoned that *Talita* must be the girl's name and Jesus was telling her to eat. After all, he had told her parents to give her something to eat.

Another misinterpretation was when one young man preached a whole sermon on the evils of smoking based on Revelation 2:6: "You hate the practices of the Nicolaitans, which I also hate." The word *Nicolaitos* in Portuguese meant to that preacher the smokers of nicotine. Hopefully, we avoided that problem by translating it as "the people who come from Nicolaita". I only hope there was such a place.

There were also many cultural problems as we struggled with the translation. "What kind of seed was it?" asked Domingos as we translated the parable of the sower. There is no general term for "seed" in Papel so we had to state what kind of seed it was. Was it wheat? Probably, but there is no term in Papel for the unknown wheat seed. Rice would be a good alternative as it is the staple diet, but no sensible farmer would ever scatter it in a way that some would fall on unsuitable ground. Each type of seed was sown in a specific way, so it would appear to the Papel that Jesus didn't know much about farming. Eventually, we found the name of a small seed that was sown by scattering that made sense in the story. It seemed a shame that we couldn't use a well-known seed like rice.

Another problem was when Jesus said, "I am the bread of life" (John 6:35). Papel people didn't know what bread was and there was no word for it, so we translated the phrase as "I am the cooked rice of life." A similar difficulty occurred with the flowers of the field. There is no general term for "flower" in Papel. We had to decide what flowers Jesus might have been referring to. Another problem was green grass. The only specific colours in Papel are white, black, and red with anything else called *fulamul*. So how could "They sat on the green grass" be translated? I scrapped the colour and said it was "pleasant grass".

There were many other difficulties with words that could not be translated accurately, such as "mountain", because Guinea-Bissau is so flat there are not even hills in the coastal area. Jesus "went up onto a mountain to pray" (Luke 9:28). I didn't question the word that Pedrinho gave me until I found that it meant "termite hill". Could I imagine Jesus sitting on the spiky top of a termite hill? So it had to be changed to ground that went up high.

Sometimes we had to be very inventive, such as when we came to Revelation 1:15: "His voice was like the sound of rushing waters." The trouble was that there are no rushing streams or rivers, and even the sea doesn't come in quickly and noisily in Guinea-Bissau. After a lot of head scratching we remembered the dykes holding back the water. To provide water a hole is drilled into the barrier and a hollow tree trunk is inserted through which the water gushes out with a loud roar – so we used that Papel word.

Part of the time I had the joy of working with Quintino Gomes, the pastor of a large, growing, mainly Papel, church on the outskirts of Bissau, where quite a number of believers were converts from Biombo. Quintino was a gifted translator, fluent in Portuguese and Creole, and he was able to express biblical truths, making them clear in his mother tongue.

However, we had a problem when we came to Revelation 3:20: "Here I am! I stand at the door and knock. If anyone hears my voice and opens the door, I will come in…" That part was easy. But then Quintino paused for a long time. "What does the rest of it mean?" he asked me.

I read again: "I will come in and eat with that person, and they with me." I couldn't see much difficulty. "We'll sit and eat together," I replied.

"The same food?" he asked. He thought again for a while and then his face lit up as he said, "I know! I understand! It means "We will both eat together out of the same gourd."

I recognized that this had such a cultural meaning. A visitor at a meal time would be given a share of the food in a separate dish and even with a spoon, if they had one. However, if a close family member or a close friend turned up he would just pull up a stool, sit, and eat with his fingers, sharing in the host's gourd.

But at times I did despair. "I'll never ever get the whole New Testament finished at this rate," I cried in desperation one day. "Oh, for a computer." Isa had a computer, so I tried to master this beast when I went to Bissau for a week – and I cried again with frustration. It was impossible. Back to the hand-writing and typing.

After the next spell of home leave I really had a problem with culture shock when I returned to Biombo. Why did it seem that everything was a problem? The heat was overwhelming and I was perpetually tired. I was working with Quintino at the time, translating Hebrews. My mind was very much on home, my friends, my church, and all the comforts and luxuries I had so recently been enjoying. We came to the verse, "If they had been thinking of the country they had left, they would have had opportunity to return. Instead they were longing for a better country – a heavenly one" (Hebrews 11:15–16). Though it was out of context God spoke to me. I was so challenged that we had to stop and pray together. There was no looking back. Jesus was all I needed or wanted.

✳ ✳ ✳

We translated the Gospel of Mark first as it was the shortest and then worked our way through Matthew, Luke, and John before moving on to Acts and the Epistles. I found Jude, the book we translated last, the hardest. It jumps about from one subject to another and it was difficult to make it flow. But it was fitting that the final verse I translated was verse 25: "To the only God our Saviour be glory, majesty, power and authority, through Jesus Christ our Lord, before all ages, now and forevermore. Amen." It just summed up our whole purpose!

So eventually, after much sweat and tears, the first draft of the New Testament was finished. It still needed a lot of checking and improving, much more than I realized then. I think I would have given up had I known all that still lay ahead.

Chapter 22

This is Not the Time to Go Home

The number of patients continued to increase during the late 1970s and early '80s, especially in the rainy season when malaria and infections were rife. It became chaotic when all the patients sheltered from the rain on the verandah of our one-roomed clinic, making any sort of a queue impossible. The two-roomed "maternity unit" usually had numerous relatives anxious to see all that went on. We allowed one relative to be present at a birth, but had a battle keeping the rest of them out.

Another problem was that the ceiling was made with bamboo canes covered with soil and palm leaves. While this kept the house cooler it was a desirable residence for the rats. They seemed to have a celebration each night, scurrying above the ceiling and dancing under the straw roof, sending soil down over the maternity beds and equipment below. The rats would also venture down at night to feed on the soap left by the plastic bowl. It became more and more obvious that we had to upgrade the building. Often, as we joined together in the early morning for prayer, we would lay this need before God. It

154

was impossible for us, but not for God, who answered our need in amazing ways.

In the short term we and our missionary team in Bissau worked together to enlarge our own little house, giving us four rooms, a kitchen, and two tiny shower rooms. What bliss! No running water yet, but that, too, came later. We began to plan in faith for a proper purpose-built building for the clinic. We had grandiose ideas and made numerous plans, imagining ourselves as architects. The only problem was money. But we and the local believers put our faith into action and began to make the mud and cement bricks that would be needed.

In late 1975 we had an unexpected and very enjoyable visit from two Tearfund leaders, Bill Latham and Tony Neeves. They must have been impressed with the work for they invited us to apply to Tearfund for help to pay for a new building. With great expectations we did, only to be told they would supply 75 per cent, or £34,000 of the funds, once we had raised 25 per cent, or £8,500. "Ah well," I sighed, knowing that was impossible, "perhaps the Lord wants us to do it ourselves more simply and cheaply."

Prayer and inconvenience went on for what seemed many months until the Lord supplied the 25 per cent needed. It came mainly through gifts from supporters in the UK, so as soon as we received the money we put in the application and it was accepted.

However, it took many months to go through all the paperwork. This gave us time to make the rest of the bricks to dry in the sun. As time passed I grew impatient, but then a miracle happened. The Guinea-Bissau government devalued the currency, so the exchange rate went from 65 pesos to 120 pesos to the pound. It was a huge devaluation. The following month the money from Tearfund came through, which was now worth almost double to us.

While all the plans were happening for the new clinic I was suddenly left alone as Brenda went on furlough, and, unexpectedly, Marjorie was called home when her mother became critically ill. By now work had begun on the new clinic. It was a building site; there were piles of stone, gravel, and sand everywhere and two trees had been knocked down. Also the government had promised to deliver 100 bags of cement, which were due any day. On top of all that there were hungry workmen, who were making the 8,500 compressed mud bricks. They were eating 4 kilos of rice per day between them as they worked in the fierce sun with their pickaxes – and for £1.40 a day each. There were still the busy clinics to look after as well.

At the same time there was work to be done on the new church. Although it was in use, windows and doors had yet to be put in, walls had to be plastered, and corrugated iron roofing from Senegal had to be installed. With the Papel conference due to start in a few days, and the heavy rains in four months, time was of the essence. After working day and night for a month, I was exhausted, and at the end of my tether. There was no missionary nurse available to move to Biombo to help me. Our field leaders, Tony and Sue Goodman, and others realized that we had no option but to close the medical work and concentrate on the building programme for a few months. They decided that I should go home to recuperate.

"How can I leave my people with no medical help?" my conscience reasoned. But the decision was taken out of my hands, so with a sense of relief and anticipation I booked a flight and wrote to tell my mother. I packed up my bags, and gave away my clothes and the little stock of food I no longer needed. I took some comfort in the fact that there was a small government first-aid post not far away which would have to cover the medical work.

Field leader Tony, Pastor Domingos, and I visited the local government administrator in his office 20 miles away to let him know of our plans, though actually we didn't need to do this. After Tony had explained the situation the administrator declared, "No, I can't allow this. Your organization must arrange for another nurse to come and continue the clinic." I waited for Tony to explain this was impossible. But to my dismay he didn't. He just agreed with the official, got up, shook hands, and walked out.

I was shocked. How could Tony say that? I was the only nurse. How could I continue to cope like this? As we walked through the door, fighting against the tears, I blurted out to Tony, "It's all right for you; you don't have to do all the nursing work." Then, leaning on the bonnet of the car, I scribbled a note to my mother, blurring the ink with tears, to tell her that I was not coming home after all.

Tony took it with him to post in Bissau while I made the miserable journey back to Biombo. As I unpacked my things, wallowing in self-pity and resentment, I again asked, "Have I no rights?" The Lord is so patient and gentle with us. A hymn we often sang in the Missionary

Training College kept coming into my mind:

> There is no gain but by a loss,
> We cannot save but by the cross.
> A grain of wheat to multiply
> Must fall into the ground and die.

I couldn't bring myself to sing it.

A week later Tony wrote to me: "We have decided that you need to have a break. Isa will go on holiday with you to The Gambia for a fortnight. We'll not say anything to the administrator." So Isa and I went. For the first few days it was no holiday for Isa as I battled with a reluctant acceptance of God's will. She was so gracious.

On the Sunday morning we went to the mission church service. The visiting preacher was a Nigerian pastor. He spoke about Jeremiah's letter to the Israelites who were in captivity in Babylon and were fretting to return to their homeland. In his sermon he repeated three times: "This is not the time to go home." I could hardly believe it. This preacher knew nothing at all about me, but my loving Jesus poured his peace into my heart. The rest of our holiday was a joy, and as a confirmation the visiting speaker the next Sunday, who was also a Nigerian, spoke about Abraham laying his sacrifice on the altar. My rights were once again consumed on that altar, and the fire of love was rekindled in my heart.

We returned to Bissau and as we got out of the car Tony met us, saying triumphantly, "We have a miracle! Tearfund is sending us two nurses and they are on the way now."

Two wonderful nurses, Helen Moules and Sally Dear, took over the maternity side completely and most of the clinic work. They loved every minute of it and they even coped with all the building work. It meant too that lives were saved that would have been lost had the clinic and maternity unit closed down.

The spacious, purpose-built clinic was eventually finished. It had six consulting rooms and a large waiting area, plastered ceilings, and a zinc roof. With the devaluation there was enough money left to enlarge the house that had been the medical centre, to put in plaster ceilings and evict the rats. It became our new spacious living quarters, possibly the finest house in the whole mission. Then the small house was upgraded to become a maternity unit – and with ceilings. When we asked Tearfund if we should return the £1,000 left over they said, "No, use it as you need it." So it went toward our second new vehicle, a Toyota Land Cruiser, to serve as an ambulance. What a miracle God gave us.

***

A new, experienced missionary, Margaret Davies from Wales, joined us. She settled in quickly, enjoyed the work, and was such a blessing to us. I was able to have more time on the translation. However, in 1980 I was called home to care for my mum who was frail with diabetes and somewhat confused after a heart attack. She shouldn't have been living alone, and as her only child I felt I must go and care for her.

I found going back to Liverpool difficult. Mum said I had to be home by 10 o'clock every night – even though

I was fifty-three years old! It annoyed me, but usually I could creep in while she slept. But one morning I found that she hadn't been asleep when I came in at 10.30 after being at a late meeting. She let me know how mean and selfish I was and she was probably right. That morning, as I was hanging out the washing on the line, I found myself taking vengeance on the clothes pegs. I was angry and resentful. Suddenly God spoke: "This is your altar, now climb on it." They were not audible words, but just as real; they were straight to my heart and I wept into a towel on the line. God provides the daily altar, but we must climb on it – every day.

For the following three months things were different. We had a lovely time together.

Interestingly, Mum had tried to dial a friend, but by mistake rang her sister, Hilda, with whom she had had a row and they hadn't spoken for two years. The situation had worried me, but God answered my prayer. That day they made their peace with each other.

One day my pastor, Ron Jones, was taking a funeral in Southport in April 1980 when he felt he should call in on my mum on his way home.

"I'm tired of being ill; I want to go," she told him.

"To go where?" asked the pastor.

"To heaven, I hope," she replied.

"Do you want to be really sure and not just hope?" he asked.

Mum, who to my knowledge had never shown any emotion throughout her life, stretched out her hand and took the pastor's hand as he prayed for her to become a Christian. The next day Mum died and a couple of months later I returned to Biombo.

Chapter 23

An Escaped Psychiatric Patient Arrives at the Clinic

The clinic continued to grow as the fame of God's needle and penicillin spread far and wide. The maternity work flourished too. We had regular ante-natal clinics, so more women had the courage to come for their deliveries, a high percentage of which were complicated. The church was growing, as forty eager Christians were now meeting every week. The believers were enthusiastic and reached out into the villages around Biombo. Each Sunday afternoon and evening they would go out in teams into different groups of houses, telling the stories and testimonies they had rehearsed in class during the week.

Life was certainly never boring. One day during the rainy season the clinic was crowded, the waiting room was full, and more than a hundred patients were still waiting under the mango trees outside. Ana Rita, our midwife, came into my consulting room and my heart sank as she said, "Miss Lily, a woman in labour has come and it isn't normal – please come."

"What isn't normal?" I asked, hoping that I could tell her I would come later.

"It isn't head first and feels like a hand," she replied. "Oh no," I thought, "not a trip to Bissau now."

She was right. The mother was in advanced labour with the foetus lying transversely. No way could she deliver normally. It would have to be a Caesarean section. To make matters worse it was twins. Both were alive, but a delay would be fatal. "I will take you to Bissau to the hospital," I explained to the mother.

"No, no, no," she said, "my husband won't allow it. I'll stay here and you will help me." We eventually located the husband, who was in the tavern and rather drunk. He was adamant that his wife couldn't go to Bissau.

"All the women die there," he said, which was a slight exaggeration. He was probably worried that if she died in the hospital he wouldn't be allowed to bring the body back for burial. Then the spiritual repercussions would fall on him, and anyway it would cost money that he didn't have.

While I was reasoning with him another patient arrived. She looked very pale and absolutely exhausted. The woman was full term, and bleeding, but not in labour. She had walked from a village 25 miles away to come to us. With her history of some earlier bleeding it was obviously a case of placenta previa (a problem in which the placenta covers all or part of the cervix), needing an immediate blood transfusion and section. "Please, Lord, help me to make it in time," I prayed.

I hurried the two of them into the car, ignoring the protests of the father of the twins, shoving him into the Toyota Land Cruiser as well. It wasn't really an ambulance, but it just held two stretchers with a tiny space between. I picked up my delivery bag, a bottle of water, a potty, some towels, and money and set off. We had gone only about 10 miles, over the deep ruts and potholes, at the top speed I dared manage, when the mother of the twins cried out, "Senhora, the baby is coming."

"No it isn't," I replied. "It can't come."

"But it is coming," she insisted, with a scream that told me that I was wrong. I stopped the car, opened the back door and squeezed in between the two stretchers. Sure enough, I could see a little bottom, and I was able to deliver the first twin, a complicated breech with extended legs and arms. It was a baby boy, probably weighing no more than 2 kilos, which, together with the bumping on the road, accounted for it being small enough and shaken up enough to turn from a transverse lie to a breech.

At least that was my theory, though it may have been a miracle! The second baby was also a complicated breech, which was delivered relatively easily. I wrapped the babies in towels, and tried to straighten my aching back. It was then I saw, through the car windows, a group of faces all watching the show. What an afternoon's entertainment for them. We had stopped on the edge of a village.

"You've got twin boys," I called out to the father, whereupon he went wild.

Apparently, the Papel believe that a man can father only one child so a second baby is either illegitimate or an evil spirit child.

"Who fathered the second child?" he demanded? "Who is the other man?" He ranted and raved, demanding an explanation from his wife. I put the placenta in the potty and sent him off to get rid of it. At that stage I didn't care where he put the placenta; the vultures would soon find it anyway. I was in a life or death situation.

The other woman now had the deep, gasping breathing of a patient dying of blood loss. Had it not been for her I would have just gone back home with the new family. For the rest of the journey to the hospital I tried to teach the father how twins are formed and how he should be very proud to be the father of two babies. I think he believed me in the end, incredible though it was to him.

We arrived at the hospital admissions department late in the evening. There was just one nurse on duty and no doctor available. Nor was there anyone to help me move the patient out of the car. The new family, with the mother walking and father carrying the twins, were sent to the maternity unit.

I got my patient out of the car and into the hospital, whereupon she collapsed. I had to drag her, unconscious, along the corridor, leaving a trail of blood behind. A man in a white overall passed me; whether he was a nurse or doctor I don't know. I asked him to help me but he replied, "Take her to the maternity ward", and just walked briskly on.

I was furious and near to tears. Eventually, the nurse on duty and I put the patient on a trolley. The man in white overalls returned, saying, "Take her back to Biombo; there is no doctor here." I was so angry.

"She will die on the way," I said.

"Phone the doctor's home," I insisted. He replied that there was no phone in the hospital; apparently it was cut off because the bill hadn't been paid. With all the authority that I could muster I sent him off to the doctor's house, saying, "If she doesn't get blood right away she will die and you will be in deep trouble."

He went reluctantly. It worried me for a long time. What more could I have done? Should I have gone with the nurse to get the doctor? If he wasn't there the nurse would have told me to take her back to Biombo. "Oh, Lord, please intervene and let her live," I prayed. I had to leave the patient at the hospital and return home.

About a week later the mother of the twins turned up to have them vaccinated. Both were doing fine. Apparently, the father had accepted the two of them and the mother was happily feeding them. This was good news indeed. Often a mother would be allowed to feed only one of twins. The one the witchdoctor declared to be the spirit baby would be left to starve to death.

A few weeks later I was thrilled to see the other woman coming into the clinic. She looked so well and greeted me enthusiastically. It was then that I found out that she was a new Christian, having been converted only a short while before she had the haemorrhage. That is why she had walked all the 25 miles to come to "Christ's house" instead of going to a witchdoctor. She told me her story. "I didn't know where I was. I was so thirsty but nobody gave me anything to drink," she explained. "Then Jesus came to me," she added, with a lovely smile.

"Perhaps it was a nurse," I said, thinking to myself, "oh ye of little faith."

"No, it was Jesus," she insisted. "He put his hand on

my head and said, 'Don't be afraid. I am with you.' Then I fell asleep and when I woke up I was in a proper bed and had a bottle of blood dripping into my arm." Apparently, a doctor had seen her the next day, did an emergency section, and gave her a blood transfusion that saved her life. She was one of the later converts in an area where we had gone many years previously. We had seen no fruit then. Now there is a vibrant church of several hundred believers.

* * *

Despite years of midwifery even I was sometimes surprised by what happened. Anna, a mum in a village half an hour's walk away, had given birth to a boy called Paulo but was still in pain. The family asked me to go out there, but it was too dark and too difficult. I asked them to bring her in on a stretcher. I also knew that I couldn't give her a proper examination with only a paraffin lamp for light in an unhygienic hut.

Some time later the stretcher arrived – but it was empty. Her husband and relatives had forbidden her to leave the hut because of all their taboos and fears. I told the stretcher bearers in no uncertain terms to return to the village and this time come back with the mother and baby. They obeyed, and when Marjorie and I examined Anna we realized there was another baby in the womb. Then, to our great surprise, we found Anna was carrying a third baby – triplets are unheard of in Guinea-Bissau. Sadly, the third triplet, whom we called Gabriel, died after a complicated breech birth, while the first baby, Paulo, lasted only a few months. But Marjorie managed to resuscitate the middle baby, Daniel, who survived. As for Anna, she became a Christian, and she and her husband, Armando Vaz, planted a church in a distant village which is now thriving.

* * *

It was wonderful how short-term volunteers and visitors came, at various times but always just when they were needed. Tearfund was so helpful sending us trained nurses and midwives. Two of those, Julia Woodford and Julia Garrood, came for a year. When Julia Garrood's parents came out to visit their daughter they kindly agreed to bring with them a couple of bulky two-way radio transmitters.

At the airport customs the police confiscated Mr Garrood's digital camera. Then we had a miracle. The police wanted to know how it worked and were so fascinated with the pictures that they all gathered round to see the show. No one examined their luggage or saw the transmitters with the 10-foot antennae being carried off and loaded into our car. We were holding our breath and praying hard. They would almost certainly have been confiscated had the police seen them, and we might have been accused of relaying political information. The police even handed the Garroods their camera back. The transmitter was a real joy and gave us daily contact with our mission headquarters in Bissau.

* * *

Another time two young aid workers from Holland were in our area and stayed with us overnight. We could hardly believe it when after returning home they raised £7,000 and then came with a team to dig two deep artesian wells; a hand-pump well for our neighbours and an electrical pump for the medical buildings.

Then Ron Harper, a WEC member from Ireland and two young men, Andrew and Mark, did a great job giving us electricity and all the plumbing. Now we had running water and electric lighting. All our neighbours came to see it and danced with joy when they saw the water flowing from their pump.

Finally, John and Jan Williamson, from Brenda's church, visited us. John worked hard laying a cement floor in the church, while Jan made some lovely cushion covers, which we filled with kapok from the local trees, for our cane furniture. We became really posh and our neighbours came round to admire them.

***

One day, when we had finished the clinic early, Brenda suggested, "Let's get away from all the interruptions and go for a picnic." I don't know why, but picnics tended to be eventful occasions; I had been on one with other missionaries and church members when I had heard that my dad had died. This picnic was also eventful, as Brenda and I packed a snack and set off with our friend Margaret Davies for an isolated and cooler place out in the paddy fields.

We had not gone far before we were followed by a group of young, mostly naked, boys. "Go home," I called out to them. No response. They just silently followed us a few yards behind. "Please go home, we've nothing for you today," I said. Still no response. We reached a grassy, shaded spot where we could see the tide coming in, and sat down, hoping to relax. The group of children had now increased to about twenty. They edged closer and closer, and stood gaping at us in complete silence. No way would they go away, and they kept looking at the bag of food we had with us. How could we eat it with all these hungry eyes staring so hopefully at us? We couldn't share a small lunch for three with twenty children. I didn't have enough faith for the five loaves and two fishes miracle in the New Testament.

I was feeling disgruntled, but Margaret solved the problem by calling the boys around her while she told them a story. They loved it. Afterwards, they all walked home happily together with us. We had our lunch at home after all.

***

Another time, when the local Christians and missionaries went for a picnic one day, I was the only nurse left in the clinic and it led to a scary episode. A man arrived asking me to come to a village 1 mile away as a woman had gone into labour, but I wasn't totally convinced by his story.

This time I set out together with Okanz, one of the believers in church who was a big man carrying a large machete and who walked between the visitor and me. When I reached the village there was no woman in labour and I was rather puzzled, as the villagers quickly hustled away the man who had called me. As there was no patient I decided to return to the clinic where, on the way, I met a worried crowd of picnickers who were desperately looking for me.

Word had soon spread that Miss Lily had gone off to a village with a strange man. What I didn't know, and what the Christians had only just been told, was that the stranger at the clinic was a very dangerous psychopath who had escaped from a Bissau prison and had killed a man. As he was a Papel he had made his way back to his home village where his family had hidden him. It was probably a good job that I didn't know at the time that hundreds of soldiers were searching for him. The prisoner was soon recaptured and taken back to the capital.

Chapter 24

Dealing with Cholera, Malaria, and Rabies

At the start of the rainy season in late May 1987 there was a severe cholera outbreak in Bissau. The government did all in its power to contain it, but there were more than 6,000 cases in eight weeks, with many deaths and a lot of fear. Cholera is a major problem in Guinea-Bissau; there had been epidemics the previous year in the north of the country, and further outbreaks would occur in 1994, 1996, 1997, 2002, 2004, and the worst of the lot in 2005, with 399 deaths.

In 1987 the road out of Bissau had checkpoints where police searched vehicles to stop bodies being taken out of the city, as in the Papel culture they believe that if a person isn't buried in his home village, his spirit will return and curse the family. The government insisted that the bodies had to be buried within twenty-four hours in a specified place in the city cemetery. But not everyone obeyed orders.

A neighbour of ours died from cholera when he was in Bissau. Two men in his family went to the capital and brought the body back in bizarre fashion. They bribed a driver and sat the corpse between them, fully dressed, in the back of the taxi. At the checkpoint the driver handed the policeman a tip, whereupon he looked through the dirty window, saw three men sitting in the back, and just waved them through. They arrived in Biombo and had the usual funeral lasting several days with crowds of relatives and neighbours making the necessary animal sacrifices and feasting. Women sat beside the corpse fanning it day and night to keep the flies away.

*** * ***

We prayed that the outbreak wouldn't spread to Biombo where sanitary conditions were appalling, especially in the rainy season, when disease was rife at the best of times. Unfortunately, the cholera did come to Biombo. Whether it was brought by our neighbours in the taxi we never did find out.

As a result government officials came and ordered that the marketplace be turned into an emergency ward. The market was simply a cemented area with no walls or roof. A government nurse was put in charge and ordered the villagers to make a fence around it.

But as there were already patients there few would go near it. However, Pastor Domingos and some of the believers went and built a fence of palm branches. Another problem was that although the nurse had bottles of intravenous saline, he had no way of suspending them, which meant they couldn't be used on the patients. So Domingos arranged a rope to be tied between trees from which the saline drips could be hung.

The situation was chaotic, as there was no equipment to cope with the copious incontinence, diarrhoea, and vomiting. Water had to be brought from the spring where people drank and where they washed the fouled clothing of the patients. Even the relatives of the patients were reluctant to help. It was an impossible job for the nurse in charge. But I am proud to say that Pastor Domingos and some believers did go down to the market on many occasions to help. Their faith in God and their care for the patients was a shining example to all.

***

We were glad we didn't have these patients coming to us. But one close friend and neighbour did come when she started vomiting.

"Please, please," she cried, "don't send me to the market; let me stay with you."

We didn't have the heart to make her go there, so we did our best. It was the most horrific nursing I have ever had to deal with – and I've seen plenty of problems. Her diarrhoea became uncontrollable and continuous. As fast as we gave her water she vomited it back. We tried to set up a drip but her veins were so collapsed that we couldn't find one, and we seemed to be losing her. In desperation we prayed and injected saline into her muscles hoping it would be absorbed, and I am delighted to say our patient recovered.

I was also worried about our staff. Hygiene was impossible. Water was in short supply, so hand-washing had to be limited too. I could only pray for protection for them, praying especially that our well wouldn't get contaminated when the nurses handled the rope and bucket. We splashed bleach everywhere until it ran out. When the outbreak was finally over we gave thanks that none of our staff and not one Christian had gone down with cholera. The well did not get contaminated either.

***

After the cholera outbreak Brenda caught malaria. This was unusual as we always took preventative pills, but they do lose their potency if they become out of date. This was a vicious attack and she was so ill her temperature soared. At 2 o'clock one morning she woke me up, carrying the Scrabble board in her hand, and saying: "Come and have a game with me." Ignoring her objections I took her temperature, which was 41 degrees. Following a lot of persuasion I put her under a cool shower and eventually got her back to bed. However, after giving her all the usual treatments she didn't improve. My best attempts at tasty food and drink were unsuccessful and every meal was a battle.

She was deteriorating fast. I was desperate and knew I had to get help. But how? The only way was to make the tortuous journey to Bissau – but would there be any help there? Still, she agreed to go. With the roads, the delays, and the heat it was a terrible journey to the hospital where I hoped to see Doctor Brandao, one of our former Sunday school scholars who was now a renowned and highly qualified surgeon. What a blow! He was away in Nigeria. As it was Friday night no other doctor was available.

We went to the outpatients' clinic where they took a specimen of blood, telling us there would be no results until Monday. Then I thought of Doctor Ingrid, a lovely Swedish Christian doctor in Bissau, so I drove Brenda to her house. Again I drew a blank. Her husband was so apologetic and explained that she was away in the south of the country and wouldn't be back until the next day at the earliest. All I could do was go to our mission headquarters and do the best I could for Brenda. I was so worried that her life was slipping away.

At around 11 p.m. Doctor Ingrid's car arrived at the mission. She had returned home earlier than planned and, although she had been driving all day on terrible roads, she came right away when she heard about Brenda. The doctor took some blood, and then diagnosed cerebral malaria and severe pneumonia, which I had missed. She set up a drip, gave her an antibiotic and anti-malarial drugs intravenously, and stayed with us for most of the night. Within a couple of days Brenda began to recover, but it was a long haul for her back to full health.

* * *

It wasn't the only major health scare. A few years earlier, one Sunday morning I was on "dinner duty" and had put some stewed fish in a hay box, a tip I'd learnt in my Girl Guide camping days. I was walking down the path to church when a stray dog suddenly rushed at me and bit my leg. I noticed that the blood was frothy, and as I looked at the dog it was running round frantically in circles, and foaming at the mouth. "Oh, no!" I thought. "That dog is rabid!"

We had had a rabid dog in the past, and we had killed it before it bit anyone, so I was no stranger to the horrific disease. Once the rabies symptoms appear it is always fatal. There is an incubation period of three to six months, which means that the disease is not usually recognized by the patient as being caused by a dog bite so long ago. We had had patients for whom we could do nothing but watch them die in excruciating agony. All this went through my mind as I went back to the house and washed the wound with disinfectant. The dog died a few days later, which confirmed our diagnosis.

I went to Bissau to try to obtain the inoculations that would, in a high percentage of cases, prevent the disease occurring. After a few days I returned to Biombo with fourteen injections to be given daily into the abdomen. Brenda, being my "private nurse", had the doubtful pleasure of administering them. By the fifth day I had developed a reaction, with a high fever, sickness, and a swollen, very red tummy. She could hardly find a clear spot to put the injection in. It got worse. So we took out the medical textbook where we read, "A reaction to the vaccine is serious, resulting in encephalitis, paralysis or death." What a choice. Feeling very miserable, I said, "I would prefer the last one."

We sat under my mosquito net that night and prayed for wisdom to know what to do – to stop the injections and risk rabies or to continue them and risk the consequences? "Please, Lord," we prayed, "show us by tomorrow morning what we should do." He did.

I slept all night and by the next morning I had no

Chapter 25

Is This the Time to Come Home?

Brenda continued to improve, recovering completely from the cerebral malaria, but Dr Ingrid said that she should have a chest X-ray – and the best place was The Gambia. As she was now fit enough to travel we combined it with a holiday and went with Helga and Meta, WEC missionaries working in other areas of Guinea-Bissau.

We felt like the idle rich, in a luxurious self-catering hotel, on a golden, palm-fringed beach with the Atlantic Ocean sparkling in the sunshine. The grounds were ablaze with red and yellow bougainvillea, hibiscus, tropical lilies, and many other exotic flowers and birds. We revelled in it all – a real bath with hot running water, a toilet that flushed, and even a floral toilet roll and a bottle of bubble bath. There was a well-stocked mini market, so we cooked bacon, eggs, and chips for tea before having a swim in the large pool. When we went to bed there was the added joy of not needing a mosquito net. We had all this for the off-season, special missionary price of £7 a day. I had forgotten how it felt to live like this.

After two weeks we were ready to return, laden with goods from the market. The journey was eventful as our ferry wasn't working. We went a long way round to another ferry and waited many hours for the tide to come in. There were some cows mooing pathetically; they, too, had been spending many hours in the burning sun. Brenda was so concerned about them that she gave them our precious water to drink; she wasn't very popular, except with the cows.

That ferry missed the tide again, so we spent the night sitting in the car. It was so hot, but when we tried opening a window a swarm of mosquitoes came in. After eventually getting off that ferry there was still miles of dirt road before another river to cross and a second ferry. It was a mad rush, and we knew that if we didn't catch the last crossing we would have to spend another night in the car.

We had heard that the boat had been ordered not to sail until a military vehicle arrived, so I was driving as fast as I could on the potholed road to get there before the military vehicle did. It was a dark, moonless night, so Brenda, who was in the front with me, was panicking that we might hit the river before the headlights revealed it. There was no such thing as a landing stage; there were no lights, notices, or signs. The road just stopped and there was the water. However, our prayers were answered and we stopped just in time. The military lorry arrived a few minutes later when we were safely aboard.

✳ ✳ ✳

It was a wonderful holiday, but we had a shock when we returned to Bissau to attend the annual missionary conferences in late 1987. It appeared that our colleagues were thinking that we were both getting older, though we hadn't noticed it. We were challenged to have a goal to hand over the medical work to the church in five years' time, by the end of 1992.

As the preacher says in Ecclesiastes: "There is a time for everything… a time to be born and a time to die, a time to plant and a time to uproot… a time to embrace and a time to refrain from embracing" (3:1–2, 5).

Yes, Brenda and I couldn't live forever. Yes, I mustn't try to hold on to what the Lord was taking from my hands. But I was sixty and healthy and I would be only sixty-five in 1992. There was no suggestion that we could work anywhere else in Guinea-Bissau, so retirement from the field was the only option. The truth was that I loved the people, the work, the excitement of the emergencies, the responsibility, and let's face it, the self-importance. Did I love my work for Jesus more than I loved him?

A verse from Madam Guyon was a challenge:

> To me remains no place nor time;
> My country is in every clime;
> I can be calm, and free from care,
> On any shore, since God is there.
> While place we seek, or place we shun,
> The soul finds happiness in none;
> But with my God to guide my way,
> 'Tis equal joy to go or stay.

Perhaps we were reluctant to let go. Brenda and I had thought much about the truth that we couldn't go on for ever. I had remarked wistfully one day, "Wouldn't it be wonderful if some wealthy American mission offered to take over the whole work and we could just move out and start again somewhere else?" She didn't go with it. Of course, I didn't either. It was just a ridiculous dream.

In the meantime there was a threefold challenge to get the church and clinic totally self-sufficient and to finish the Papel translation of the New Testament. But as we thought about training a leader and a team capable of running the clinic and maternity unit without any missionary input, and under the management of the church, we knew we were asking the impossible.

How could the struggling Guinea-Bissau church, in all its poverty, provide the tens of thousands of pounds that were needed each year? There was also the small matter of finishing the translation work which I thought was under my control. Then, to my utter dismay, just after I had done a lot of work in checking and improving the first draft, I heard that the Bible Society would now take on the publishing of new translations only if they were computerized. I was devastated. It seemed the end of a futile road. I couldn't even attempt it. I gave up and wallowed in self-pity.

We had no option but to accept the challenges of the clinic, the church, and the New Testament translation and admit that we had a God who did the impossible.

Chapter 26

An Angel Arrives as a Computer Crashes

Once the decision to leave was made so the build-up to 1992 started and the miracles began to happen. First, I received a letter from one of our missionaries in Bissau, Ursula Pasut, a German lady who is a brilliant linguist. "Lily," she wrote, "I will come to Biombo and put your New Testament on the computer."

She couldn't do that, I thought, knowing that she didn't speak or understand any Papel. I told her that it was a nice thought, but quite impossible. Ursula wasn't put off by my lack of faith. She came and worked solidly for more than two months until the whole Papel New Testament was keyed in. Later, when it was checked, I found her typing was virtually faultless. Secondly, a lovely English friend, Sally Shand, came for two weeks in March 1992 and taught me more about using the second-hand elderly computer that I had been given.

***

Plans for the church and the clinic were also going well. The church in Biombo was mature under the good leadership of Pastor Domingos and several presbyters, deacons, and deaconesses. It was growing steadily, although quite a few of the young converts went off to the city to study or to work. This added considerably to the Papel church in Bissau, but didn't help the one in Biombo.

However, the leaders were managing their church finances without any direct help from us. Tithing, that is, giving a tenth of one's income to God, was taught and faithfully practised, but it was mostly in eggs and tomatoes so very little money was handled. In reality, their income and expenses were pathetically small.

As for the clinic the newly appointed Romao Lopes seemed the ideal leader. He was a qualified nurse, having trained in the Bissau hospital, and a keen, mature Christian eager to serve God using his skills. Although he wasn't a Papel he was respected by the missionaries, the church, and the patients.

But we needed to train him and his team so that they could run the clinic on their own when it was handed over to the Guinea-Bissau church on the agreed date of 4 July 1992. Tearfund sent Audrey Fernandes to oversee the whole training project and we were grateful for the excellent way she did this. We arranged for Romao to go to England for three months to learn English to help him with the correspondence and with the business side of the clinic. Also, along with Tiago and Tito, he learned to drive.

Then we gave the two trainee midwives, Ana Rita and Celeste, more responsibility and they too rose to the challenge. When a team from a Youth with a Mission

(YWAM) ship gave Tiago some training we were delighted that the dental work we began could also continue. This was followed by a team from the Christian Blind Mission (CBM), who trained other team members in some aspects of ophthalmics so that the eye care work we set up could carry on.

The church elders in Bissau were enthusiastic about taking over the responsibility of the medical work, but they were blissfully unaware of all that this would entail. They formed a committee of five, who would be responsible for frequent visits and supervision. There didn't seem to be any thought of money, nor did they want to discuss it.

We decided that it would be easier if we spent the last six months in Bissau working on a literacy project and let the church and clinic get used to being independent. We had two official send-offs, and my eyes were filled with tears on both those memorable days. On Saturday, 27 June the church and medical team invited us to a "little banquet" in the clinic waiting area which had been filled with benches, plastic bowls, large pans of rice and pork, and dozens of tins of orange juice. The church president and lots of people came from Bissau, plus members of the Biombo church and many missionaries. There were gifts of chickens, eggs, and vegetables in abundance.

On the following Saturday, 4 July, the church laid on a sumptuous feast of chicken stew and rice and orange juice when several dignitaries came, including the Guinea-Bissau Minister of Health and her team plus the national TV and radio teams. The minister was very friendly, but as we stood in the queue to get our meal I made the mistake of trying to talk to her in my rusty Portuguese. "Have you any children?" she asked.

"I'm not married," I explained in my best Portuguese, and then, waving my arm over the gathered crowd, I stupidly added, "I have a great family and many children here." To my horror she looked shocked, having taken me literally. I had a problem talking my way out of that. I would have done better speaking in Creole.

There were the usual speeches for such an occasion and then we were each presented with a beautiful, colourful, hand-woven cloth, each with our name and "Biombo" woven into it. Finally, Audrey Fernandes, on behalf of the mission, officially handed over all authority to Romao, though she agreed to stay on as an adviser for three months until she flew home to England on 4 September. It was all such a wonderful, precious, and priceless expression of the love of the Biombo people for us. How privileged we had been.

We enjoyed our last six months in Bissau, though we missed the activity, the sense of being needed in Biombo, and the fellowship of the team there. But there were advantages of being in the capital, such as fresh bread and vegetables outside our gate and well-stocked shops. An unexpected benefit was that we could buy cheap season tickets for the Sheraton Hotel where we could enjoy their superb swimming pool – a different world to that outside the hotel.

* * *

But then just as everything was going well, my whole world collapsed. It was August – and only four months before Brenda and I were due to fly home – when I suddenly lost everything on my computer. Whatever I did, in my abysmal ignorance of this monster machine, I don't know, but all my Bible translation work disappeared.

In fact, the beast stopped working altogether. Nobody could help me sort it out, not even Isa. I was distraught! I could have thrown my computer in the sea. "Dear Lord," I cried, "is all that work lost for ever? Should I have attempted this translation at all? If I'm to continue I need a miracle. Please!"

One evening, a few days later on 29 August, I was back in Biombo for Audrey's farewell when a stranger came to the clinic. He was a white, tall, very blond, handsome man, probably in his thirties. We invited him for tea and the Dane explained that he had come on behalf of his wife who was in Bissau undertaking research on "Sanitation in rural Africa" for UNICEF, the United Nations Children's Fund. She hadn't the time to come to Biombo to complete her research so he had come instead.

"What can you tell me about sanitation here?" he asked.

We smiled and said, "That's easy; there is no sanitation. Everyone finds his or her own special tree that gives some sort of privacy, except for the tavern owner and two or three others who have dug a privy." We answered a few more questions and then he explained that he worked in computers, solving problems, but there was hardly any work for him in Bissau.

My heart leaped in anticipation! "Oh please," I begged, "could you look at my computer?" I explained what I was doing and eagerly showed him my problem.

However, it was late afternoon and he needed to return to Bissau. "I am sorry," he said. "I think I could fix it, but it would take some time and we are leaving for Denmark tomorrow." What a disappointment. I could have wept, but I tried not to show it as he seemed so sorry. I wondered why the Lord had let him come at all to build up all my hopes and then to have them dashed so quickly.

But early the next morning he appeared again, walking up our path having left Bissau around 5 a.m. I thought he looked like an angel as he sat there at my computer for several hours, working silently all morning, his blond hair shining in the sunshine. He eventually called me over to show that the computer and printer were working perfectly and all my New Testament work was there, restored. What a miracle! The day before I could have wept; now I could have danced with joy.

"I must rush off now," he said. "My wife will be anxious. We fly later this afternoon."

I offered to pay him but he refused so we gave him a little African hand-painted picture. To this day I can only remember his Christian name, Forma. I sometimes wonder – was he an angel? But angels don't have wives, do they, and are they computer experts? However, he certainly was an angel to me. I suppose he will never know, in this life, what a vital part he played in giving the Papel tribe the New Testament in their own language.

Chapter 27

Another Amazing Answer
to Prayer

Brenda and I flew home to England just before Christmas 1992. Although it was the festive season we had difficulty settling back in to life in the UK. Both Brenda and I missed Biombo: the comradeship, the excitement, and the sense of being needed. I felt that I was "on the shelf" – a very comfortable shelf, but nevertheless, a shelf. For years we had lived in an open home, with visitors coming and going all day. We hardly ever had an uninterrupted meal. Now life was so much quieter, monotonous, and boring, but we soon became involved in our home churches. Our bodies may have been in England, but our hearts were still in Guinea-Bissau.

Any hopes I had of sending off the New Testament manuscript for publishing when I was back in the UK were soon dashed. I found that there had to be much more checking with the Bible Society's consultants and then the typesetting. Thankfully, Wycliffe came to my rescue and I was able to work with their expert typesetter, going over each book of the Bible again and again. In all it kept me busy for almost two years.

I had three consultants, one based in Senegal, another in the USA, and the third in England, who carefully checked every book. "How did you translate that passage?" I was asked on many occasions. They knew all the difficult ones to translate, but on the whole I didn't have to change too much.

Even so, despite all the experts checking the work, one embarrassing error nearly got through. I was re-reading 1 Timothy 3:12 where it says that an elder should be the husband of only one wife. The word for only, *soo*, was missing in the printout I had received from Wycliffe so I wrote the word by hand in the margin in red ink, pointing out where it should be inserted. When I received the corrected manuscript back again from the typesetter, who of course didn't understand Papel, I thought I had better check everything one final time before it was printed. I found he had read "soo" as "500". It now said, "An elder should be the husband of 500 one wife."

When the New Testament was finally printed in Papel Brenda and I were invited to Bissau for the dedication ceremony, which was a real highlight with missionaries and Christians coming from all over the country for the service. I was delighted when the Bible Society consultant, Dr Phil Stein, came from Senegal to be present. He, in particular, had been such a help and an encouragement to me.

***

I returned again to Guinea-Bissau for a few weeks in November 1995, to give some literacy classes to the pastors and leaders from the various Papel churches. I was very moved when I went to the Sunday morning service in our Biombo church. As I approached the church there was loud singing, clapping, and drumming. The church verandah was crowded with people looking in through the windows while another group was standing in the doorway. What a sight greeted me. I stood for a moment in utter amazement. I thought of when I had stopped at the church on my way to the clinic each morning, so many years ago, when I spent a few minutes praying for what seemed then an impossibility: "Please, Lord, may this church be really full of believers praising you one day."

Now I was seeing the answer to my prayers. It was more than full. I was overwhelmed. Tears of joy and thankfulness flowed freely as I walked down the narrow aisle between the packed benches. There was a loud chorus of hallelujahs, disturbing the colony of bats that hung upside-down on the rafters, who all woke up and fluttered around angrily, but nobody seemed to notice or care. In front of the platform a crowd of children were squashed together on mats. I was invited on to the platform to speak, but I could only raise my hands and choke out, "Thank you, thank you, thank you, Lord."

Yes, we felt satisfied. God was blessing the church. Pastor Domingos was an ideal pastor who served God with all his heart. The Papel New Testament was now available. Although not many people were able to read it, literacy was increasing which meant that those who could read Creole could read Papel with a little extra instruction.

***

We were also delighted that the clinic was continuing to run efficiently. Romao was a wise and respected leader. Financially, the clinic kept afloat with gifts from Brenda's and my church and other friends, and I was able to order and supply from England all the medicines that were needed.

But, I wondered, did we then rest on our laurels during the next few years? Did we forget that we were in a battle zone? We perhaps should have seen the warning signs earlier. We discovered that members of the committee, which the church leaders in Bissau had appointed, were disappearing. Dr Brandao went to another country, a missionary went home, others lost interest, and one had died, so there were no visits and no supervision of the clinic. Then, sadly, Romao had to leave for disciplinary reasons. This was a terrible loss as there was no one to replace him.

Tiago and Tito worked faithfully carrying the load, with just occasional short-term help from Bissau, but things deteriorated further. We were no longer able to give money through the mission, and what money we did send through another channel, which the church had requested, was often swallowed up by what was considered to be a more urgent need than the clinic in Biombo. Thankfully, I was still able to send medicines, through the kindness of a businessman in Bissau, Yan Van Mannen; otherwise the clinic would have been closed down.

The staff carried on as best they could, but sometimes they received no salaries. Then the two excellent midwives left. First Celeste married her fiancé, Bilopat, who now lived in Portugal. Ana Rita was severely injured when a tree fell on her, and she went to Portugal for treatment where she stayed long-term.

The future for the clinic was grim. I began to wonder – was the Lord showing us that the time to close the medical work had come? Treating the people with God's needle and penicillin had been the key to opening up the area and planting a church that was now thriving and independent. Was the medical centre no longer necessary? If it closed down would the government start something else in Biombo? That was very unlikely. The evangelical medical centre was a definite plus, as it gave the mission credit in the eyes of the government. Closing it down would be a bad witness and possibly go against us.

Of course, we recognized that medical work was by no means essential in most missionary endeavours. There was ample proof of that in Guinea-Bissau. Several tribes had been evangelized and many churches established by sharing the gospel alone or with other social activities, and the churches were growing. God doesn't need our abilities as much as our availability and obedience. He has many ways of working – even through a needle.

***

We didn't know what to do as there seemed to be no clear answer to our prayers.

Then God called Loida Patrao, a lovely older woman and a keen Christian, who had worked with missionaries in Bissau. She had trained and qualified as a nurse in the hospital in Bissau before taking on the leadership of the clinic. It was a costly undertaking as the conditions were poor and money was scarce.

Over the next two years Loida did well, working hard and holding everything together, but with a diminished staff and no trained midwives she was hopelessly overworked, and sometimes out of her depth. The situation continued to deteriorate. The vehicle needed expensive repairs and was no longer running; the generator had "died" because of lack of maintenance. That meant they were back to candles at night and water from the old well with a bucket and rope. Any repairs to the buildings, such as mosquito screening and painting, were out of the question, as any available money had to be spent on food.

They were not helped by the political situation. The Commissioner for Armed Forces, Nino Vieira, who had overthrown Luis Cabral in a bloodless coup on 14 November 1980, decided in June 1998 to halve the size of the army. A group of rebels seized strategic locations around the capital, including the airport, and demanded Vieira's resignation. When Senegal and Guinea sent troops to support Vieira's regime civil war broke out and 250,000 residents fled the capital, some of whom came to Biombo. After fierce fighting, in May 1999 rebel leader Brigadier Ansumane Mané gained power, and Portugal granted Vieira political asylum.

We were very sad to hear of the country's plight and disappointed to see the clinic and maternity unit at such a low ebb. Had all our hard work in building up the clinic and maternity unit been in vain? "Lord, we need a miracle," we prayed. But we didn't imagine the miracle he would give us – and that we would have to wait seven years for the answer.

✳✳✳

In autumn 2006, Ernesto Lima, a much-loved elder and statesman in the Bissau City Church, began to take an interest in the struggling Biombo clinic. He prayed much about it and tried to encourage the staff. He named the centre "O Bom Samaritano" (The Good Samaritan). He wrote to me and mentioned that two Portuguese ladies had done some painting there in September that year. Whatever did he mean by this? There had never been any Portuguese women in Biombo and whatever would they want there?

The mystery deepened when I had a phone call from a Portuguese woman, Olinda Pedroso, saying that she and Mena Almeida and another friend wanted to visit us in England for a weekend. I went to the airport to meet them, expecting to see three older women all dressed in black, because that is how I remembered typical older Portuguese women from my time in their country. Or maybe they were nuns? I was anxious about my rusty Portuguese which had never been very good. Would I be able to talk to them? I had such a surprise when they appeared. They were younger than me, wearing jeans and T-shirts, and spoke very good English. The trio were warm, friendly, and chatty and I felt an immediate rapport with them. Olinda and Mena were both voluntary helpers with a Portuguese Catholic non-political and non-religious relief organization that was working in Guinea-Bissau. They had been for two weeks to visit Biombo to look into starting a school. It didn't happen, so they were at a loose end.

As they surveyed the villages, they came across the Evangelical Church and the medical centre, and met some of the believers. Olinda and Mena were impressed with their friendliness and were happy that Pastor Domingos and a few others could speak some Portuguese. The women were taken round the clinic and maternity unit, but were shocked to see the dilapidated buildings and the broken-down equipment, all of which showed that it had once been an efficient, working medical centre. They were surprised that the small team were still treating patients as best they could, despite all the difficulties.

Olinda and Mena decided that, for the rest of the time in Guinea-Bissau, they would do something about it. They went to Bissau, bought paint, brushes, cleaning materials, sheets, towels, and sponge mattresses to replace the old stained ones, and set about painting the clinic. The women heard about the church, the beginnings of the clinic, and the exploits of Miss Brenda and Miss Lily, and returned to Portugal fired up to continue helping the people of Biombo. They wanted to meet with us to sound out the possibilities. We had an exciting weekend with them talking over the joys and problems and seeing their enthusiasm to take on the challenge of resurrecting the clinic. Could this be the answer to our prayers? We introduced them to the leaders in our churches and discussed this new venture with them. Olinda and Mena stressed that they wanted to take the clinic on as their own personal project, not under the jurisdiction of the organization they represented. However, that organization proved to be very helpful. Olinda and Mena were ready to consult the leaders of the Evangelical Church in Guinea-Bissau first and get their approval. It all seemed so way out and unpredictable, yet there was a deep sense that God was in it. We could only wait and trust.

* * *

Olinda worked full-time in Portugal, while Mena owned and ran a restaurant. How could they take on such a commitment, as well as having their homes and families to consider? Yet only a short time later they went to Guinea-Bissau to make a start. They gained the full and very eager approval of the Bissau Church Council and then went to assess the priorities in Biombo, which included a new generator and a new car.

What followed is almost beyond belief! The following January they took their holidays and returned to Biombo with a team of twelve volunteers including doctors, physiotherapists, a dentist, a pharmacist, and other gifted helpers. They had already shipped out a container-load of equipment and medicines. For two weeks everyone worked hard cleaning, painting, and renewing the furnishings. The lack of facilities – water from the well, candlelight at night, the long-drop toilet with its cockroaches, bathing under the stars – didn't faze them. In fact, they enjoyed it so much that most of the volunteers returned the following year, and all at their own expense. Two container-loads were sent in advance of that visit, including more equipment, furnishings, and, wonder of wonders, a new ambulance and a new generator. The pump on the well was repaired and a water tank installed. The pharmacist created a pharmacy and a woman dentist set up a dentistry in one of the clinic rooms, complete with a proper dentist's chair. A delighted Tiago was given more training and equipment and was designated "The Dentist".

Back home the women raised money for their project by holding Christmas bazaars and other fundraising events. Their work attracted national attention and they appeared on Portuguese TV. For the Biombo staff it meant that they could be paid and that the clinic could have a complete makeover.

* * *

In 2007 I was delighted to be invited by the Portuguese women to go out to Biombo with them so that I could meet all the helpers and see for myself all that had been achieved.

I was absolutely amazed to see the transformation in the clinic and the maternity unit. The buildings had all been repaired and painted. As I walked from room to room and saw the refurbishment and improvements I could only wonder at the amount of hard work and expense that had gone into it all. So many willing, enthusiastic people had been involved. Who but our faithful God could have orchestrated all this? What a wonderful illustration of love from this group of Portuguese volunteers to the people of Biombo.

The clinic had been wonderfully upgraded. A legacy from a friend of mine provided for both the clinic building and the church being re-roofed and a good wire fence erected around the property, and there were plans for a new maternity unit.

It was obvious that the medical centre must become self-supporting. Being considered foreign aid workers (NGOs), Brenda and I were not able to charge the patients anything, but that wouldn't apply to the national church. Olinda and Mena were now getting the patients accustomed to paying something toward their medicines. The pharmacist had tabulated the medicines, marked the pricing, and had been teaching some accountancy to the staff. Also I was delighted to see the well-stocked and orderly medicine cupboards.

I went to the Sunday morning service in the church. It was a wonderful welcome and so very moving to meet all our faithful friends again. Some looked so much older, but then so did I. But I was surprised to see that, although the church was full, with every bench occupied, there were not the crowds that I had seen on a previous visit.

"How is it," I asked, "that there are fewer believers here now?"

"Miss Lily, it's wonderful now," they explained. "God has answered our prayers. People used to have to walk here from Blom, Bisa, Quepedo, and other villages a long way away, but now they all have their own churches." What more could I ask!

But there was more. A couple of years later Wycliffe Bible Translators invited me and Thelma Mills, who had worked as a translator in the Balanta tribe, to return to Guinea-Bissau to work on dubbing the *Jesus* film into the Papel and other languages. I had three keen and helpful Papel believers working with me. We worked long hours in spite of a rather severe flu epidemic with diarrhoea and vomiting that hit our little group, but nobody missed a session. The film is now available in Papel and much used.

***

As I look back on my life I am so thankful for the privilege of being chosen to start the clinic in Ondame that treated so many patients and saved the lives of many mothers and babies. I was privileged to be there at the beginning of the Biombo church where hundreds of Papel became Christians, some of whom are now leaders in the national church of Guinea-Bissau. I was honoured to be involved in writing down the Papel language for the first time and translating the New Testament so the people could read God's word in their own language. All this had started with the wonderful gift of God's needle and penicillin. To Him be the glory.

Appendix 1

Whatever Happened to…

After reading a book or seeing a play, many people want to know what became of the characters and tie up the loose ends. Here's what happened to those involved in taking the gospel to the Papel tribe in Biombo, Guinea-Bissau. I have listed the people and organizations in alphabetical order.

Audrey Fernandes is married to Mark Skinner, whom she met in Bible School, and they are now missionaries with Wycliffe Bible Translators, overseeing translation work in Senegal and Guinea-Bissau.

Betty Dutch died in October 2003. Lily and Brenda were with her in the hospital when she passed away.

Biombo church in Ondame and in other surrounding villages continues to grow and thrive.

Brenda Couche died on 24 April 2011. Lily and her niece were with her in hospital. She left Lily a note saying, "I'm going on ahead of you but you'll soon be following me. Hallelujah!"

Good Samaritan Clinic in Biombo continues to function with the help and oversight of the Portuguese ladies and their team of volunteer medics and helpers who visit every year. They are in the process of building a new purpose-built maternity unit.

Lily Gaynor is living in her bungalow, Pleasant View, in Prescot Road, Melling, Liverpool, L31 1AR, speaking at meetings as and when requested and keeping involved in her church.

Loida Patrao is still the head nurse in charge of the clinic and has another government trained nurse assisting her.

Margaret Davies moved to work in Empada in the north of Guinea-Bissau, then worked as the hostess in the WEC Headquarters in Bissau. She is now retired, living in Swansea.

Marjorie Gowland left Guinea-Bissau in 1984 and returned to Gateshead where she met Robert Broughton at a WEC prayer meeting. They married on 16 February 1985, and Marjorie took Robert to Guinea-Bissau to show him where she had been working. Robert died and Marjorie is still living in the North East.

Pastor Domingos Gomes died a few years ago. His wife Amelia also died more recently. Their son Tito is a leader in the church in Ondame and chief nurse at the clinic.

Thelma Mills has finished the translation of the Balanta New Testament and is now retired, living in Southampton.

Appendix 2

The Biggest Challenge of Being a Missionary

"Helen," I said, "if someone asked you what your biggest challenge was, as a missionary, I guess you would say finance, wouldn't you?"

"Oh no," she answered, and there followed a conversation that I have never forgotten.

It was during my first term when I had spent several extremely hard, stressful months caring for the little children and babies in our Garden of Happiness in Bissau, while Helen McKenzie, a senior missionary, was off sick. It was particularly stressful because money was so short. I was certainly relieved when Kathleen took over until Helen returned to take charge again.

"No," Helen had replied thoughtfully, "money isn't a problem. My problem has always been to keep the fire burning in my own heart."

Helen's wise words have lived with me, as I have found again and again that it has been, and still is, my biggest problem. Finance for God's work, worrying though it may be at times, is God's problem and not mine. However, it is my responsibility to keep the fire burning in my heart.

What is the answer?

I have had to keep coming back to Leviticus 6:8–14, where a vital truth is hidden in a difficult book to read. Three times in seven verses it says, "The fire must be kept burning", and it tells us how. First is the clearing out of the ashes each morning. The tiny particles of ash that clog the fire are like the little, unrecognized sins of thought and word that need daily confessing and clearing away.

At one time Brenda and I realized that we were becoming habitually critical, so we decided not to say anything about anybody that we wouldn't say if that person were present; and we would prompt each other when needed. Brenda had no difficulty with it, but I did. I found I had no conversation. What was more I resented the promptings. There were many other things too that dulled the fire, each small and apparently insignificant in itself, but together they would stifle the flames and put it out.

Second is the need for daily fuel. Not all wood is good fuel: some will just smoke; other wood will put a fire out. I learned that when, on one occasion, I had helped to gather firewood for our women. They had great fun, laughing together and saying to me, "This piece would make my eyes stream with the smoke. This piece would send sparks and set the straw roof on fire. This piece would put the fire out." All the wood looked acceptable to me and I thought I was being helpful. We need to be discerning in what we take in, what we read or watch or relax with, and the time-consuming things that are of little value spiritually. Aren't we so blessed with the availability of the best fuel – our Bible?

Third is the whole daily sacrifice. The whole purpose of the fire is to consume the offering. A daily dying to self, our rights, our pride, our comforts, and all the many things that go to make up our ego. It's a daily taking up of the cross, not just to carry it but to die on it.

Who'd ever be a missionary?
By Lily Gaynor and a WEC short-termer

There are weevils in the flour and crawlies in the rice,
Rats are in the cupboard and the dog is full of lice.
Chickens sneak in the kitchen, the birds eat all our corn,
The frogs prefer the bathroom where it's always wet and warm.

The pigs get in the garden, and cows are in the church,
On the rafters up above them a hundred bats all perch.
Frogs are croaking in the night and crickets on the bleep,
Rats are gnawing in my room when I want to get to sleep.

Cockroaches scurry in the drawers, the plastic bags all spoil,

They chew up Brenda's cookery book to nest in
    tubes of foil.
Mosquitoes biting in the night, and jiggers in
    my toes.
A blockage in the septic tank, I could do
    without my nose.

Puddles in the labour ward, I get in such a flap,
The mop head's gone quite baldy and no water
    in the tap.
Post-natal full to bursting, can't take in any
    more,
Granny's sleeping in the bed, mum and baby on
    the floor.

Guava, orange, lemon trees, we've fruit of every
    type
But all of it is stolen before it's ever ripe.
Who'd ever be a missionary and who would ever
    stay?
Lord, give me grace to laugh a bit and just get
    through today.

Appendix 3

Whose Story is It?

Is it the story of Pastor Domingos Gomes, who, together with other early believers, founded the Biombo church? Yes.

Or is it the small group of Papel Christians who prayed fervently, believing that God would answer and give a harvest, who carried on working when it seemed impossible? Yes.

Or is it the story of the little medical team who faithfully battled on, continuing to work when they felt deserted and everything seemed hopeless? Yes.

Or is it the various helpers who came for short or long periods just when they were needed? Yes.

Or is it our churches and friends in England who gave sacrificially, making it possible to buy the medicines, including the penicillin, and pay the wages running into many thousands of pounds? Yes.

Or Tearfund, who responded to our need of help? Yes.

Or the Bible Society and Wycliffe, who made it possible for the Papel people to have the New Testament in their own language? Yes.

Or the whole team of volunteers from Portugal who have been the means of resurrecting an almost dead medical centre? Yes.

Or the faithful prayers of so many who have prayed through the years? Yes.

Or is it the story of our Lord Jesus who has saved us, guides and prepares us and gives all of us the privilege of serving him? He gives forgiveness in our failures, strength in our weakness, joy in our work, and meets our every need. **YES?! YES! YES!**

For all of God's promises have been fulfilled in Christ
with a resounding "Yes!" And through Christ, our
"Amen"… ascends to God for his glory.
2 Corinthians 2:20, NLT

Publish His glorious deeds among the nations. Tell
everyone about the amazing things He does.
Psalm 96:3, NLT

AMEN